RETRIEVER HUNT TESTS

A Handler's Guide to Success

James B. Spencer

Alpine
PUBLICATIONS

Crawford, CO

Retriever Hunt Tests: A Handler's Guide to Success

ISBN 10: 1-57779-093-6
ISBN 13: 978-1-57779-093-8

The information contained in this book is complete and accurate to the best of our knowledge. All recommendations are made without guarantee on the part of the author or Alpine Publications, Inc. The author and publisher disclaim any liability with the use of this information.

For the sake of simplicity, the terms " he" or "she" are sometimes used to identify an animal or person. These are used in the generic sense only. No discrimination of any kind is intended toward either sex.

Cover Design: Laura Newport
Editing: Deb Helmers
Layout: Laura Newport
Photographs: All photographs by the author unless otherwise noted.

1 2 3 4 5 6 7 8 9 0

Printed in the United States of America.

TABLE OF CONTENTS

To my wife, Theresa,
Who will surely get a high place in heaven
For putting up with me and my dogs for all these years.

ABOUT THE AUTHOR

Jim Spencer has been involved with retrievers since the late 1940s and with hunt tests since their beginnings in the early 1980s. In 1983, he covered the first UKC/NAHRA hunt test for *Gun Dog* magazine. In 1985, he judged the Master level in the first licensed AKC retriever hunting test and has since judged all three levels (Junior, Senior, and Master) of AKC hunting tests. He has also judged the highest level (Finished) of UKC/HRC hunts and the upper two levels (Intermediate and Senior) of NAHRA field tests.

He has campaigned his own retrievers at all levels of AKC hunting tests. He is currently running his Golden Retriever, "Gamble" (KC's Take'n A Chance, MH). He has also campaigned spaniels in and judged all levels of AKC spaniel hunting tests. His English Spring Spaniel, "Flick," (Orion's Flicker, MH) was one of the early MH spaniels. He has campaigned his German Shorthaired Pointer, "Erick" (Westwind's Erick Von Grief, MH) through all levels of AKC pointing breed hunting tests. Jim has conducted retriever and spaniel training seminars all across the country.

Since early 1986, Jim has written the "Retrieve" column for *Gun Dog* magazine, and the "Retrievers" column for *Wildfowl* magazine since mid-1985. He is the author of the following books, all of which are available from Alpine Publications, Inc.: *Training Retrievers for Marshes and Meadows; Retriever Training Drills for Marking; Retriever Training Drills for Blind Retrieves; Retriever Training Tests; HUP! Training Flushing Spaniels the American Way;* and *POINT! Training the All-Seasons Birddog.*

Jim says that, since May 22, 1954, he personally has been trained and handled by his wife, Theresa, who has relied on "totally positive re-enforcement." He leaves it up to others to decide whether that system worked satisfactorily in this case. They have five grown children.

PREFACE

At first I thought about calling this book, *Your First Hunt Test: Things "They" Forgot to Tell You!* That title would suggest the contents of the book rather well. Whenever a person takes up a new hobby, whether it's dog games, golf, poker, pool, or whatever, he can read and study as much as he wishes, but he won't find everything he needs to know in the extant literature. Some things you have to learn the hard way—that is, by making mistakes, by watching others do things right, and by asking perhaps too many questions. In my rather long life, I've taken up more hobbies than the average person, so I've gone through this hard-way learning process often enough to be exceedingly familiar with it. It's frustrating and wastes too much time and often too much money. For example, learning the hard way in hunt tests costs a person in entry fees and travel expenses. This may be cheaper than learning to play poker the hard way, but it's still very expensive...and unnecessary.

The literature of every sport seems to have gaping holes here and there, and the unsuspecting beginner falls into most of them as he struggles to become proficient. My own early frustrations in the retriever sports have led me to write books that fill in at least some of those gaps. I call them "niche" books, because they fit into a previously empty niche in the literature.

My first niche book was *Retriever Training Tests* (initially published in 1983 by Arco; the second edition is available from the publisher of this book), a book to help the beginner understand how to set up effective tests for training his retriever. In a sense, this book was a bit of an accident, in that I started out to write a training manual. But I found myself putting test designs at the end of almost every chapter. It finally dawned on me that there were already several good training manuals, but not one single book on how to set up tests. So I pulled the test designs from each chapter, added many more, explained them more thoroughly, and turned the results into a separate book, unlike any retriever book I'd ever seen. In the preface, I pointed out that it wasn't a complete training manual. Although most reviews were glowing, a couple of reviewers, apparently failing to grasp the niche book concept, focused their reviews on that one statement in the preface, treating it like a warning on a product label. In other words, they reviewed mostly what the book isn't, a training manual, and never mentioned what it actually is, an in-depth tutorial on test design. Happily, that book is now twenty-two years old and still in print, so their tunnel vision didn't do it any serious harm.

My second and third niche books were born as "fraternal twins." I started to write a book on training drills for retrievers because that seemed to be another huge gap in the literature. About halfway through the writing, I realized that it would work better as two normal-sized books rather than one huge one. I contacted the publisher, Betty McKinney, and told her I was hearing two heartbeats. She agreed that it should be two books, and thus was born *Retriever Training Drills for Marking* and *Retriever Training Drills for Blind Retrieves* (both published in 2001 by Alpine Publications). These have been well received by their intended audience, neophyte retriever trainers wanting to improve their training programs with better drills.

And so this is my fourth niche book. It addresses a wide gap in the literature concerning effective handling in hunt tests. All really experienced hunt testers know how to handle retrievers in these events, but no one has compiled this wealth of information for the struggling beginner. Until now, that beginner has had to pick it up the hard (and expensive) way. In judging hunt tests, I've seen so many green and "under-informed" handlers mess up their dogs one way or another! As a matter of fact, the reason I never wear whistles while judging is that I fear I might, without realizing what I was doing, blow the *Sit*-whistle to stop a dog that some inexperienced handler is allowing to get into serious trouble. I get too emotionally involved with each handler and dog team when I'm judging. I once came very close to tossing my judging book in the air in a surge of frustration when a green handler blew a totally unnecessary *Sit*-whistle—his dog was doing beautifully and needed absolutely no help. This handler then proceeded to (mis)direct his dog into more and more trouble, all because of that initial, unnecessary *Sit*-whistle. You might say that he blew the whole test with that one whistle.

Incidentally, I changed this book's title because even the most experienced and skillful hunt test handler needs an occasional refresher course. We all tend to become careless at times, especially after a series of successes. We so easily and so unconsciously slip into bad habits that must be identified and rooted out. That is true of all sports—that's why touring pro golfers take lessons from time to time. Therefore, this book is addressed to hunt testers at every level, not just beginners. We *all* need periodic refreshers. In fact, I'll probably pick this book up myself occasionally and read certain parts that address handling problems I may encounter now and then. I've certainly done that with my other three niche books.

The Structure of This Book

This book contains three sections, each with two or more chapters.

Section I, "Overview of Hunt Tests"

Chapter 1, "What Are Hunt Tests?" explains the essential features of hunt tests: namely, that they are noncompetitive, that they simulate hunting, that they have four sponsors (AKC, UKC/HRC, NAHRA, and CKC), that they have three graduated levels of testing, and that they offer meaningful titles to successful retrievers.

Chapter 2, "The Origin of Hunt Tests," gives a brief history of the early days of the hunt test movement, which began in the early 1980s.

Chapter 3, "Hunt Test Popularity," shows statistically how hunt tests have grown in number of events, number of entries, and average entries per event.

Chapter 4, "The Challenge of Hunt Tests," shows statistically the level of difficulty for a dog to qualify in each level of each hunt test format.

Section II, "Successful Handling"

Chapter 5, "General Preparations," explains how the beginner should prepare for hunt tests from the day he decides to participate until he leaves home to run his dog in his first actual event.

Chapter 6, "General Handling Guidelines," offers general advice for handlers while they are participating in a hunt test, covering such things as exercising and airing the dog, feeding and watering the dog, listening to the judges' instructions, watching the test dog, going to and leaving the line, getting the callbacks, and attending the awards ceremony.

Chapter 7, "Marking Tests," offers specific "at the line" advice for handling a dog in single, double, and triple marking tests.

Chapter 8, "Blind Retrieve Tests," offers specific "at the line" advice for handling a dog in single and double marks, combination marks and blinds, and how to deal with various distractions and hazards.

Chapter 9, "Other Types of Tests," offers advice for handling a dog in upland hunting and tracking (or trailing) tests.

Section III, "Addenda"

Chapter 10, "Putting on a Hunt Test," explains what a retriever club must do in order to put on a successful hunt test.

Chapter 11, "So You Want to Be a Judge" encourages newcomers to aspire to judging if it interests them and offers a couple of cautions that should, if heeded, help them become good judges.

The book ends with a brief Appendix listing the contact information for the four organizations (AKC, UKC/HRC, NAHRA, and CKC) that sponsor hunt tests.

How to Use This Book

Each of us has his own approach to learning from books. Let me suggest my own, which you can use as is, modify here and there, or totally disregard, depending on your own tastes and experiences.

First, read the book from cover to cover rather rapidly. This will give you an overall grasp of the material it contains and a general idea of where everything that especially interests you is. Then, go back and reread those sections that deal with your current situation relative to hunt test handling. If you've just acquired your dog, focus on Chapter 5, "General Preparations." If you will be entering your dog in a hunt test anytime soon, focus on Chapter 6, "General Handling Guidelines," and the relevant sections of Chapter 7, "Marking Tests," Chapter 8, "Blind Retrieve Tests," and Chapter 9, "Other Types of Tests." If you've been running your dog in hunt tests with reasonable success for some time now and are beginning to think about judging, focus on Chapter 10, "Putting on a Hunt Test," and Chapter 11, "So You Want to Be a Judge?" And so on.

From time to time during your years of hunt test participation, go back and reread the chapters that are especially relevant for you at the time.

As I said, this is just my approach to "book learnin'." I'm a book nut who has been a dedicated reader since early childhood. Books have always been my favorite sources of information and entertainment. As you can see, since I never really finish reading a good book, I really get my money's worth from books—and my library is full of good ones!

I hope this book will serve you well as hunt test participant, as handler, as worker, and as judge.

James B. Spencer

SECTION I

Overview of Hunt Tests

Chapter 1
What Are Hunt Tests?

In the retriever world, the generic term "hunt test" includes four quite similar programs. The American Kennel Club (AKC) sponsors "hunting tests" for retrievers. The United Kennel Club (UKC), through its subsidiary Hunting Retriever Club (HRC), sponsors "hunts" for retrievers. The North American Hunting Retriever Association (NAHRA) sponsors "field tests" for retrievers. Finally, the Canadian Kennel Club (CKC) sponsors "hunt tests" for retrievers. Although each of these programs is unique in some ways, they share enough essential characteristics to allow a person to run one retriever in all four of them, if he so chooses. This chapter describes those common traits and explains why they are so important for retriever folks.

NONCOMPETITIVE

Most importantly, all four formats are noncompetitive testing programs. Each entered retriever is judged against a written standard. Each dog either passes or fails based on his own work, not on how his work compares with that of the other dogs entered. Thus, when you enter your dog in a hunt test, you needn't worry about what poker players call the "good second-best hand syndrome," in which you come away empty even when your dog has one of his better days, as so often happens in competitive dog games like field trials and dog shows. In hunt tests, if your retriever does the work, he passes, period. It doesn't matter if several other dogs do significantly better work. It doesn't matter how many dogs pass or fail.

This lack of competition has important benefits. Perhaps the most obvious is financial. You can win whatever hunt test titles you aspire to by simply having your dog do the work the required number of times. For example, if the title you seek requires, say, five "passes," or qualifying scores, you can earn that title in as few as five hunt tests. In field trials, where points toward titles are awarded competitively, you might run a very good dog that is working well in trial after trial after trial without earning a point because your dog's work is never quite good enough, given the competition. Running a retriever in either hunt tests or field trials costs significant money, of which entry fees are the cheapest item. Training (whether personal or professional), travel, motels, and restaurants really run up the bill. In hunt tests, if your dog is well prepared for whatever title you seek, you can predict the cost of acquiring that title with reasonable accuracy. Not so in field trials, where you don't know what the competition will do from trial to trial.

Because hunt tests are noncompetitive, participants tend to be more relaxed and friendly. Since they don't have to beat one another to succeed, each handler can cheer for every other handler from the bottom of his heart. In any competitive situation, those who are still "in the hunt" cannot help hoping that the others who are also still in the hunt fall by the wayside. After all, if all the others don't falter, how can one win? Thus, in any activity, competition breeds some level of animosity among participants (although in civilized societies it's often—but not always—hidden behind outward signs of friendliness). A professional dog show handler once told me that, whenever he was *not* winning regularly, he had lots of friends at every show, but when he had a dog that was picking up lots of pots, the atmosphere became quite chilly.

Compared with that of competitive dog games, the atmosphere at hunt tests is quite refreshing. Most participants are sincerely friendly and mutually supportive. Of course, a few have such intensely competitive natures that, no matter how well they do, they can't feel truly successful unless they feel they have "defeated" everyone else in some way or another. In "casual" conversations, such a person endlessly and ad nauseam compares his dog's work with that of other dogs—and somehow his dog always come out on top. If his dog had sloppy marks but good blinds, the handler focuses on the other dogs' blinds, and vice versa. Happily, at hunt tests, such insecure bores are few and easily avoided. Besides, they don't usually last long.

Since hunt tests are noncompetitive, the judges don't have to make their tests more and more difficult in order to find a winner. In a field trial, the judges have about a day and a half in which to run at least four series that will not only separate the sheep from the goats but also allow them to rank the top four sheep for placements. Since entries are huge in most stakes, the judges can complete their assignments on time only by making the trial an elimination contest, in which they drop from one-third to one-half of the dogs after each series. To drop so many dogs, most of which are professionally trained, the judges must set up progressively more and more difficult tests, not only within a trial, but from trial to trial and from year to year. And as the judges invent new and more difficult tests, the professional trainers figure out how to train for those tests. Thus the judges must tax their ingenuity more and more for each judging assignment. Sometimes they pull old and almost forgotten tests from their memories, but mostly they invent new and more difficult ones.

In hunt tests, the judges need only determine which retrievers can and cannot do the work expected at each given level. If all of them do the work, the judges can pass them all. If none of the dogs do the work, they needn't pass any of them. Of course, the usual situation falls somewhere between those two extremes. But to complete their assignments properly, the judges need neither eliminate dogs ruthlessly nor rank the survivors. Thus, they needn't make their tests more and more difficult from series to series, hunt test to hunt test, year to year.

That said, one cannot deny that, in the highest level of each program, the difficulty of tests has been increasing during the past few years. This is for two reasons. First, many field trialers run their dogs in and judge hunt tests, which is wonderful as long as they leave their competitive-event mindset at home. Unfortunately, not all of them do. Second, as will be explained below, each format offers strong incentives to continue running dogs after they have earned the highest level titles. These incentives consist of additional, highly prestigious titles and annual or semi-annual big-deal invitational events.

Because of these most attractive incentives, many dogs with highest level titles continue to run in regular hunt tests year after year. These "old hands at the game" necessarily elevate the overall average performance in the highest level of each format. This, in turn, encourages judges (at least subconsciously) to increase the difficulty of their tests. Even so, the rules of each format are specific enough to prevent this from getting out of hand, as it does in competitive dog games.

HUNTING SIMULATIONS

Partially as a reaction to what many consider artificiality in field trials—extremely long and complicated tests, white handler jackets with black gloves, visible white-clad gunners, and so on—those who designed our four hunt test formats drew up rules that mandate true simulations of actual hunting. Perhaps the most obvious change from field trials is the attire of all hunt test participants: Judges, workers, and handlers all must wear hunting or hunting-like clothing. You will see lots of camouflage at any hunt test you attend.

Retriever hunt tests prepare retrievers for hunting.

The most practical aspect of these "real-life" regulations is that they limit the distance of tests. AKC limits all tests in all testing levels to a maximum of 100 yards. UKC/HRC limits its lowest level tests to 75 yards on land and 60 yards in water, its middle level to 100 yards on land and 75 yards in water, and its highest level to 150 yards on land and 125 in water. NAHRA limits its lowest level to 75 yards on land and 50 yards in water, its middle level to 100 yards on land and 75 yards in water (except that the water blind may not exceed 50 yards), and its highest level to 100 yards for all tests, land and water. CKC limits its lowest level tests to 75 yards and its middle and highest level tests to 125 yards (and preferably 100 yards).

Frequently a newcomer complains that these maximums are much longer than his dog's typical retrieves while hunting. However, when you consider how far some lightly hit birds fly before falling, in both waterfowling and upland hunting, you realize that these distances don't exceed practical hunting distances. In fact, the very existence of maximum lengths forces judges to think in terms of realistic hunting retrieves. Then, too, because you know what these distances are, you can plan your training program more efficiently, unlike field trialers who sometimes face tests so long that they need field glasses (really!) to see their dogs.

Each hunt test format calls for extensive use of normal hunting equipment: large decoy spreads, boats, realistic duck and goose blinds, the use of various game calls (duck, goose, pheasant, whatever), plenty of shooting, and hunting clothes for all participants. In the early days, this "realism" sometimes got way out of hand. Back then, I witnessed one test that looked and sounded as if a duck calling contest had broken out in the middle of a reenactment of the Battle of Gettysburg, with the battlefield relocated to the shores of a lake so crammed with decoys that the dogs had trouble finding water in which to swim. Fortunately, those early extremes eventually yielded to more practical hunting simulations.

To better simulate hunting, the upper two levels of all formats involve diversion shots, diversion birds, walk-ups, and so forth. Bird throwers are normally hidden from view, unlike field trials where they wear white jackets and stand out in the open. Before throwing, they attract the dog's attention by blowing a game-bird call or firing a shot.

Then, at the top of the bird's arc, they fire again, perhaps more than once. In all formats, handlers in the upper two levels must carry and point shotguns at each bird. In UKC/HRC hunts they must fire popper shells at each thrown bird. In the highest level of all formats and in the middle level of AKC, UKC/HRC, and CKC tests, each retriever must honor while another dog works.

Before the test dog runs at the start of each series in every level, the judges are expected to give a "hunting scenario" as an explanation of the test to the assembled handlers. This encourages handlers to show up at the start of each series, thereby eliminating unnecessary delays all through the test. It also enables handlers to learn what the judges are seeking, to ask questions, to see the test dog's performance, and to hear the judges' comments on that performance. Then, too, it forces judges to justify their tests in a believable hunting framework, and it gives them the opportunity to answer questions from handlers. In the early days, it unfortunately gave a few exhibitionists a captive audience before which they could demonstrate their theatrical skills...or lack thereof. Some of these early judges spent more time explaining and demonstrating (with dramatic strides, gestures, and voice tones) their hunting scenarios than it took for several dogs to run the actual test. After spectating at some of these seemingly endless performances, I found myself wondering whether the performer wanted to be a judge or a Shakespearean actor. (In some cases, I found myself doubting that the judge had ever actually been hunting.) Happily, those days are behind us. Today, judges explain their scenarios quite quickly and matter-of-factly.

MULTIPLE LEVELS

Each hunt test format (AKC, UKC/HRC, NAHRA and CKC) has three graduated testing levels. This allows each person to enter his dog with reasonable hopes for success in a level appropriate for the animal's current training and experience. It also encourages each person to continue training in order to progress from one level to the next.

The lowest level (AKC and CKC "junior," UKC/HRC and NAHRA "started") suits the talents of a dog with only a modicum of training and experience. It consists of four or five single marked retrieves, at least two of which must be in water. All formats require a reasonable level of steadiness. The AKC and CKC formats require delivery to hand, but UKC/HRC and NAHRA do not.

The middle level (AKC and CKC "senior," UKC/HRC "seasoned," and NAHRA "intermediate") demonstrates the talents of a working retriever of the typical hunter, the good ol' meat dog. It consists of two double marks (one on land, one in water) plus two blind retrieves (one on land, one in water). In addition, the NAHRA intermediate and CKC senior include an upland hunting test. All formats require steadiness and delivery to hand. AKC and CKC require honoring.

The highest level (AKC and CKC "master," UKC/HRC "finished," and NAHRA "senior") shows off the high-gloss polish of an accomplished trainer's dog, the retriever of every hunter's dreams. In all formats, the tests include two or three multiple marks (typically triples), with at least one in water, plus two or three blind retrieves, again with at least one in water. The CKC master includes an upland hunting test. The NAHRA senior includes an upland hunting test and a trailing test. All formats require steadiness, delivery to hand, and honoring.

MULTILEVEL TITLES

For retrievers that succeed the required number of times in each level of each format, the sponsoring organization awards a title and a frameable title certificate. These titles are permanently recorded in the sponsoring organization's record books and placed in the dog's pedigree. Like the other AKC and CKC noncompetitive titles, the AKC and CKC titles for each level go after the dog's name in the pedigree. The NAHRA and UKC titles, like all their other titles, go before the name in pedigrees.

Lowest Level Titles

At the lowest level, AKC and CKC award the title "Junior Hunter" (JH) to a dog that qualifies in four of their respective junior level hunting tests. UKC awards the title "Started Hunting Retriever" (SHR) to a dog that passes four UKC/HRC started level hunts. NAHRA awards the title "Started Retriever" (SR) to a dog that qualifies in four NAHRA started level field tests.

🦆Middle Level Titles

AKC and CKC award the title "Senior Hunter" (SH) to the dog that qualifies in four or five (depending on whether he has a JH title) of their respective senior level hunting tests. UKC awards the title "Hunting Retriever" (HR) to the dog that passes in three or four (depending on whether he has an SHR title) seasoned level hunts. NAHRA awards the title "Working Retriever" (WR) to the dog that qualifies in three or four (depending on whether it has an SR title) NAHRA intermediate level field tests.

🦆Upper Level Titles

At the highest level, AKC and CKC award the title "Master Hunter" (MH) to the dog that qualifies in five or six (depending on whether he has an SH title) of their respective master level hunting tests. UKC awards the title "Hunting Retriever Champion" (HRCH) to the dog that passes six to ten (depending on whether he has SHR and HR titles) UKC/HRC finished level hunts. UKC also awards the title "Upland Hunter" (UH) to the dog that passes four UKC/HRC upland hunts. NAHRA awards the title "Master Hunting Retriever" (MHR) to the dog that qualifies in four or five (depending on whether he has a WR title) NAHRA senior level field tests.

🦆Extra Titles

As mentioned above, each sponsoring organization awards additional titles to dogs that meet further requirements after earning the respective highest level titles. While it isn't yet an official AKC title, owners of dogs that qualify in the annual AKC Master National Invitational Hunting Test frequently add the title "Master National Qualifier" (MNQ) after their dogs' names in pedigrees. The Master National Retriever Club (MNRC) awards the after-the-name title

"Master National Hunter" (MNH) to dogs that qualify twice in the AKC Master National Invitational, and enroll in the MNRC Hall of Fame (with the title letters "HOF") dogs that qualify three times. CKC awards the before-the-name title "Grand Master Hunter" (GMH) to dogs that, after earning the MH title, qualify in ten additional master level hunt tests. UKC awards the before-the-name title "Grand Hunting Retriever Champion" (GRHRCH), to the dog that, after earning the HRCH title, either passes in fourteen additional UKC/HRC finished level hunts or qualifies in two semi-annual Grand Hunts. NAHRA awards the before-the-name title "Grand Master Hunting Retriever" (GMHR) to the dog that, after earning the MHR title, qualifies fifteen additional times in NAHRA senior level field tests.

SIGNIFICANCE OF HUNT TEST TITLES

The presence or absence of these noncompetitive hunt test titles on pedigrees greatly simplifies two important processes: a breeder's selection of appropriate breeding stock and a hunter's selection of promising litters of puppies.

Before these titles were available, a breeder had to rely on field trial titles, personal experience, and word-of-mouth reports to help him determine which dogs should be bred. However, field trial titles have always been so extremely difficult and costly to acquire that many people with outstanding retrievers don't even try. Thus, before hunt tests, a breeder could evaluate the working ability of many dogs in a pedigree that lacked field trial titles only by personal experience or trustworthy word-of-mouth reports. Because both personal experience and reliable reports were so often lacking, many worthy dogs without field trial titles were never bred.

The national breed clubs sponsoring each retriever breed has long had a "working certificate" or "working dog" program, with after-the-name titles (WC, WCX, WD, WDX, WDQ, and so forth) designed primarily to demonstrate the working ability of show dogs. These vary from club to club, but they do give some information about the dogs that have these titles. However, few owners outside of the dog show world run their dogs in these events, or even understand what the

titles mean. Thus, they haven't been much help to the average breeder of hunting dogs. However, CKC has implemented a very meaningful working and widely understood certificate program in which the
titles (WC, WCI, and WCX) require work similar to (but simpler than)
the corresponding CKC hunt test titles (JH, SH, and MH).

Hunt test titles have added a series of standardized, well-under-
stood, and truly significant titles. A breeder can now evaluate pedigrees quite accurately from the presence or absence of hunt test
titles, especially in the first three generations of the dog being studied.
If those fourteen dogs have titles, the breeder can tell exactly what
performance level each one has achieved. If a given dog has a JH, an
SHR, or an SR, he has done single marks on land and in water. If he has
an SH, an HR, or a WR, he's a really fine hunting retriever, capable of
double marks and single blinds on land and in water. If a dog has an
MH, a HRCH, or a MHR, he's a dream dog, capable of triple marks and
double blinds on land and in water. The CKC SH and MH and the
NAHRA WR and MHR also indicate ability in upland hunting. The
NAHRA MHR further indicates trailing ability. The other titles, MNQ,
GRHRCH, GMHR, and GMH, are more prestigious but require roughly
the same level of work as the MH, HRCH, and MHR. If a given dog in
the first three generations of the pedigree has no hunt test titles, no
field trial titles, and no working certificate titles, his working ability
should be seriously questioned (unless the breeder either personally
knows otherwise or can learn otherwise from reliable sources). The
more questionable dogs a breeder finds among the first fourteen in
the prospective dog's pedigree, the less likely he will be to use that
dog for breeding. Frankly, now that hunt tests have been around for
over twenty years, most retriever breedings should be between titled
dogs whose pedigrees are heavily laced with titled ancestors, especially in the first three generations.

Similarly, hunt tests have made it possible for a prospective puppy
buyer to evaluate the performance potential of each litter whose pedigree he studies. The above breeder's rules apply for this process, too.
Look at the first three generations, in which you'll find fourteen dogs.
If those fourteen forebears are properly titled (field trials, hunt tests,
or certain working certificate tests), the litter should have good field
potential. The more untitled dogs you find among those fourteen, the

weaker the breeding appears to be. Of course, if you know something about an untitled dog from personal experience, you may be able to overlook his lack of titles. But beware of rave reviews from the breeder or his friends.

Also keep in mind that, no matter how royally bred, every puppy is a gamble. You do increase your chance of hitting the jackpot, however, if you insist on proper titles for the first three generations of the litter from which you choose your puppy.

HUNT TEST AS A HOBBY

Although hunt tests have many practical aspects for breeders, puppy buyers, and hunters in general, they have become extremely popular primarily because they are so enjoyable as a hobby. They encourage participants to train frequently and intensely. They encourage the formation of simpatico training groups within retriever clubs. They offer a series of achievable and progressive goals to all participants. They encourage people to get active in the outdoors. And, most of all, they're fun in and of themselves.

Chapter 2
The Origin of Hunt Tests

UNITED STATES

A "noncompetitive American sport" sounds like a contradiction in terms, doesn't it? Traditionally, we Americans have been a fiercely competitive people. Some would say this trait approaches a national mental illness, while others would point to the many outstanding contributions American competitiveness has brought to the entire world. Take your choice. Strangely enough, we developed this competitiveness from Calvinism, a religion that had widespread influence in the American Colonies. Back in the 16th century, the Frenchman, John Calvin, built his new religion on the theory of "pre-destination," which claims that God has pre-destined only certain people (the Elect) for heaven and that everyone else, that is, the majority of all people, necessarily for hell. Calvin also taught that God blesses the Elect with prosperity in this life, and that the Elect can therefore be recognized by their earthly prosperity. When Calvinism crossed the English Channel, it became Puritanism, the form in which it reached our shores and spread throughout the Colonies. Clearly, American Puritanism combined with freedom and seemingly limitless opportunities for prosperity, inspired a strongly competitive spirit among our country's early settlers. Ironically, this American competitiveness continues to thrive today, long after both Calvinism and Puritanism have largely disappeared.

So how did noncompetitive hunt tests ever get started here, and why have they become so extremely popular? Frankly, it's just one of many happy results stemming from the massive post-World War II explosion of the American middle class. Within the retrieve world, our field trials couldn't accommodate—in fact, had never been designed to accommodate—such an explosion.

🦢Retriever Field Trials

The first AKC retriever field trial was held by the newly formed Labrador Retriever Club, Inc. (LRC), in December 1931, at the estate of Mr. Robert Goelet near Chester, New York. LRC's founders and initial officers were among the American economic aristocracy of that day: Mrs. Marshall Field, Mr. Robert Goelet, Mr. Wilton Lloyd-Smith, Mr. Averill Harriman. During the 1920s, many wealthy Americans visited English estates to hunt birds in the English manner, where the breed of choice was the Labrador Retriever, which had surpassed the Flat-Coat in popularity shortly before World War I. Gradually, these Americans began importing Labs and Lab trainers from the British Isles so they could simulate English shoots on their American estates. That led to the development of AKC field trials. Two facts should be painfully obvious here: First, these folks weren't concerned about the cost of competing in their newly developed program; second, since they started field trials during the early years of the Great Depression, they had no reason to make provisions in their program for middle-class participation, since the middle class was then minuscule, and nothing suggested that this situation would ever change.

From the earliest days, professional trainers dominated retriever field trials. Initially, they were the full-time employees of the few wealthy Americans who created these trials. Later, after World War II, when the middle class began to grow and prosper, more and more pros went into business for themselves, each training for a number of upper-middle-class clients who were wealthy enough to pay for their services but not wealthy enough to hire them full-time. Thus, because of pro domination, field trials have always been fiercely competitive and highly expensive.

Most people in that rapidly growing middle class were unable to comfortably afford professional training, even though they had been able to afford hobbies that were beyond the financial reach of their parents and grandparents back before World War II. Many of this new, moderately affluent middle class took up hunting with retrievers. Some even tried training their own dogs for field trials, but few were able to beat the pros. Over the years, a growing group of retriever owners spread throughout the country, a group that needed an off-season dog game requiring less commitment of time and money than field trials. Many blamed field trials and field trialers for not providing them with the opportunities they sought. This was totally unjust, of course, because those who developed and maintained field trials did so for their own recreational purposes, not as a benevolent service to mankind in general. Nevertheless, after World War II, frustration and the resulting anti–field-trial sentiment grew at about the same rate as retriever popularity. By the early 1980s, it was strong enough to become a movement.

THE HUNT TEST CONCEPT

The late Richard A. Wolters, in the May/June 1982 issue of *Gun Dog* magazine, launched that movement with a "Retrieve" column titled, "The Gun Dog Stake." In it, he described a Gun Dog Stake that the James River Retriever Club had recently held. It was a three series stake with many just-like-hunting trappings, such as retrieves within reasonable hunting distances, handlers carrying shotguns, real duck blinds, lots of decoys, calls, and so forth. Like regular field trial stakes, this was a competitive event. Mr. Wolters proposed that readers storm the powers of AKC to incorporate this type of competition as an additional stake in their licensed field trial program. Please note that his proposal didn't eliminate the one factor that caused field trial tests to become ever more difficult, ever more pro-dominated, and therefore ever more expensive. That factor, of course, is competition. Mr. Wolters proposed the new gun dog stake be just another competitive field trial stake, but with a number of just-like-hunting features.

Actually, what he proposed wasn't all that new. Many retriever clubs around the country had been having "hunter stakes" and "gun dog stakes" in their fun trials for years. In my local club, the Jayhawk Retriever Club, pro trainer Dean Campbell had introduced such a stake into our monthly fun trials back in the early 1970s.

Nevertheless, for American retrieverites, Mr. Wolters' column was the "shot heard around the world." Readers responded in great volume and with great enthusiasm. Mr. Wolters had a natural flair for promoting whatever interested him. Thus, in the pages of *Gun Dog* magazine, he eventually refined his single-level competitive gun dog stake into the three-level, noncompetitive hunt test format—including the appropriate titles—that we have today. He also organized the North American Hunting Retriever Association (NAHRA) to conduct these tests, under the name of "field tests." We cannot thank him enough for the energetic way in which he promoted this program.

None of the ideas he incorporated were new—far from it. For many years, most AKC-affiliated national breed clubs sponsoring our various sporting breeds had been offering noncompetitive "working certificate" or "working dog" tests, some of them with two and three graduated levels, and all of them awarding titles to go after the dogs' names in pedigrees. One of these programs, that of the American Chesapeake Club, was remarkably similar to what our hunt tests became. Then, too, the North American Versatile Hunting Dog Association (NAVHDA) had been conducting multilevel noncompetitive tests, with titles, for versatile (pointing) dogs for decades. Obedience trials, which started in this country shortly before World War II, have three progressive levels with noncompetitively earned titles. Also, most European countries have had noncompetitive field-testing programs with titles for perhaps a century. Thus, no one involved in the development of our hunt test programs can rightly claim to have invented any part of them.

🦊 My Involvement

I began running my dogs in field trials in a small way back in the late 1960s. Small way? Oh, yeah, really small. As a middle-class husband and father of five, I couldn't afford to play with the big kids in the major stakes. But instead of becoming frustrated and bitter against trials, as so many did, I simply set lower, more achievable goals for myself. Instead of aspiring to the major stake titles, I sought only to turn one of my dogs into a "Qualified All Age" retriever, which can be done by placing first or second in a Qualifying Stake, one of the minor stakes the big kids ignore. In 1977, I succeeded in doing this with my home-bred Golden, Rumrunner's Brandy***. Although happy with that small accomplishment, I really wanted to earn a title that goes on pedigrees. But field trials offered nothing within my reach.

Back in the 1950s, I had earned noncompetitive titles in AKC obedience trials. Although the judges award four placements in each obedience class, placing isn't required for the titles. To earn an obedience trial title, a dog need only qualify three times at the appropriate level. After Brandy's success in 1977, I found myself wishing I could earn a title in a noncompetitive dog game that was field-related, with a format similar to that of obedience trials. I tried the working certificate tests of the Golden Retriever Club of America, in which I later earned a WC title with my Golden, Patton Manor's Benedictine, WC. But I wanted something more challenging, more meaningful.

In the 1980-81 time frame, I wrote my first book, *Retriever Training Tests*, which—as often happens with books—wasn't published until 1983. I ended that book with the following plea for noncompetitive, title-giving formats for both field and show:

> *It is too bad that the obedience format was developed after the formats for field trials and dog shows. Had the reverse been true, these latter two might have offered noncompetitive titles, as does the truly effective obedience format. Whether such titles will ever be available remains to be seen. I hope they will.*

When I wrote this, I had no idea that, by the time the book would come out, the new hunt test formats, which would answer the field half of this plea, would be well along in the planning stage.

In 1982, after reading Mr. Wolters' "The Gun Dog Stake" column, I wrote an article titled, "The Gun Dog Stake—Where Now?" and submitted it to Dave Meisner, then the owner/publisher/editor of *Gun Dog* magazine. In this article, not surprisingly, I recommended a field-testing format similar to that of obedience trials. In short, I said it should be noncompetitive, should have three progressive testing levels, and that titles should be awarded to dogs that pass a given level three times.

On November 12, 1982, Mr. Meisner responded as follows:

> *Dear Jim:*
>
> *Bear with us on a reply concerning your article, "The Gun Dog Stake—Where Now?" Copies have been sent to Dick Wolters and our associate editor. After they've had a chance to review it and comment, I'll get back to you.*
>
> *Dave*

He didn't get back to me for over six months! On June 24, 1983, he wrote:

> *Dear Jim:*
>
> *I'm afraid that "The Gun Dog Stake—Where Now?" is no longer timely. Since you wrote the article, Wolters and a group of other people have been formulating a Hunter's Retriever Club which will sponsor what we've been calling the Gun Dog Stakes. There will be mention of this in our July/August issue and we expect to have a significant announcement regarding it in our September issue.*
>
> *Dave*

At the time, I was disappointed that my article wasn't to be published. But I figured that the new program Mr. Wolters was cooking up had taken an entirely different course and that my article would therefore have been somehow counterproductive. But later, when I read that Mr. Wolters and his associates had put together a field-testing program that was quite similar to the format suggested in my unpublished article, I felt ill-used.

Looking back on it, I guess it really doesn't matter, and for a couple of reasons. First, Mr. Wolters and his group developed a wonderful format, regardless of where they got their ideas. Second, as I said above, none of these ideas were original with any of us, for they were present in the format of not only obedience trials, but also of working certificate tests, NAVHDA tests, and a number of European field tests. Even if I had never written that article, and even if Mr. Meisner had never sent a copy to Mr. Wolters and his group, they would have heard these ideas from many other sources and would have surely developed the same outstanding program.

As I said, we can't thank Mr. Wolters enough. At that very critical time, he stepped forward with the talent necessary to select the really good ideas from the many suggestions he must have received. Then, too, in addition to recognizing the good ideas, Mr. Wolters displayed a great and badly needed talent for promoting the hunt test program, which he did so very successfully through both *Gun Dog* and NAHRA.

✤ The First UKC/NAHRA Hunt Test

After formulating a program, NAHRA felt they needed to associate with a respected registry in sponsoring their field test program, so they formed an alliance with the United Kennel Club (UKC). Together they conducted the first UKC/NAHRA sanctioned field test September 24-25, 1983 on the J. D. Blondin quarter horse farm near Arcadia, Louisiana. Dave Meisner asked me to go there and cover the event for his *Gun Dog* magazine. My story ran in the November/December 1983 issue.

In the two lower levels (started and intermediate), the clubs ran all three series simultaneously, setting up different tests in three different areas, each with its own judge. After finishing the first test, the handler took his dog to the location of the second test, ran it, and then proceeded to the third and final test. Nice concept, but it took lots of ground, lots of judges, and lots of workers, so clubs haven't been able to continue using it. In the highest level (master), they ran the first two series simultaneously, and then ran the third and final series separately after all dogs had completed the first two.

Since this was the first-ever hunt test of any format, I'll describe the tests briefly. Fortunately, I still have a copy of my *Gun Dog* story ("NAHRA Showcase and a Rebel Yell," November/December 1983), so I don't have to rely on memory. The started level consisted of three single marks: first, an eighty-yard land dove simulation; second, a sixty-

The welcome sign at the first UKC/NAHRA hunt test, held September 24th and 25th, 1983 near Rustin, LA.

A realistic blind used in the first UKC/NAHRA hunt test.

A level 2 land mark in the first UKC/NAHRA hunt test.

A level 3 walk-up land mark in the first UKC/NAHRA hunt test.

yard land dove simulation; and third, a thirty-five-yard water duck simulation with a real duck blind and lots of decoys—a test in which they threw a live, shackled duck that sometimes crawled off into cover and hid, forcing the dog to hunt for it.

The intermediate level started with a land double mark, with the falls at sixty and seventy-five yards. Next, they had a land walk-up with a pigeon flushing from a remote release trap a short distance ahead of the handler and dog, with two live gunners shooting it. The third series was a water double mark, from a real duck blind, with each duck falling at about fifty yards into a stump-studded, decoy-filled pond. In the intermediate level, the handler had to shoot a shotgun loaded with popper shells at each bird.

The master level tests were quite interesting. First, they ran a land double mark (dove simulation) with the falls at about seventy and fifty yards, with a flier diversion bird shot from near the line as the dog returned with his second retrieve. The handler sat on a stool and shot popper shells at each bird. The second series was a walk-up with two birds flushed from remote release traps to fall on the far side of some heavy cover at about twenty-five and thirty yards. Again the handler had to shoot popper shells at each bird. The third series was a water double mark at about fifty and thirty-five yards, with an interesting twist. The memory bird was attached to the line on a fishing rod and reel and was thrown out into open water. As the dog retrieved the go-bird, the hidden memory bird throwers reeled the memory bird duck back into their blind and tossed a dead duck off to the side. This forced the retriever to track the thrown bird up the shore before he could find the tossed dead duck. Here, too, the handler had to fire a popper load at each bird.

Incidentally, for any history buffs among you, the judges were as follows:

> *Started:* Chris Kilgore (first series), Troy Scallion (second
> series), and Ron Greer (third series)
> *Intermediate:* Chip Rainwater (first series), Mark Morgan
> (second series), and Paul McLaughlin (third series)
> *Master:* Bob Rathe (first and third series) and Bill Tarrant
> (second and third series)

The test chairman, genial host, and mastermind of the entire operation was pro trainer Omar Driskill of Rustin, Louisiana.

As you almost certainly noticed, this first hunt test had no blind retrieves and no triple marks (unless you consider the diversion bird in the master level the third bird of a "delayed triple"). UKC/NAHRA had not yet fully developed the rules, so the judges at every level focused on simple but realistic everyday marking situations. After the rules were fleshed out more fully, they included blind retrieves in each of the upper two levels and triple marks in the highest level.

Shortly thereafter, NAHRA broke off from UKC and formed an alliance with AKC. UKC formed the Hunting Retriever Club and initiated their own UKC/HRC hunt test format, called "hunts." The NAHRA/AKC alliance didn't last long and each proceeded to develop its own format, AKC "hunting tests" and NAHRA "field tests." Thus, by the end of 1984, in United States, three separate organizations were sponsoring, or at least planning to sponsor, quite similar hunt test programs: AKC, UKC/HRC, and NAHRA.

The First AKC Hunting Tests

On June 8-9, 1985, two retriever clubs held separate "first" AKC-licensed hunting tests. One was the Jayhawk Retriever Club in Kansas, and the other was the Lufkin Retriever Club in Texas. Unfortunately, I have no written report on either of those events, so I'll have to rely on my memory. I can't recall most of the judges, but Jim Reid and I judged the master level for Jayhawk and Eddie Rathburn was one of the two master level judges in Lufkin.

Back then, the AKC master level format included, in addition to the usual non-slip retriever tests, an upland quartering test and a tracking test. Wanting to make sure the entered handlers knew

The Master Level judges for the first licensed AKC retriever hunting test held by the Jayhawk Retriever Club on June 8th and 9th, 1985: Jim Spencer on left, and Jim Reid on right.

what truly great quartering looked like, I invited Chad Betts to run a couple of his field trial English Springer Spaniels as test dogs in these two series. Wow! Did they put on a show! (I should add that in 1991 when I judged a nearby AKC-licensed spaniel hunting test, I invited Perry Overstake to bring his field trial Labrador to run as test dog for the spaniel master level water blind. Hey, fair is fair, right? Again, wow! Did he put on a show! Overall, the reaction of the retriever folks in 1985 was much more positive than that of the spanielites in 1991, a few of whom were so outraged that they refused to watch the Labrador test dog run!)

At this initial 1985 Jayhawk retriever hunting test, the late Bob Bartell attended as the AKC representative. Before the first series began, he called the six judges together and preached a vigorous sermon to us about not turning this into an elimination contest by dropping lots of dogs after each series. He stressed that this was a noncompetitive hunting test in which we didn't have to find a winner. That sermon was highly effective. Jim Reid and I carried most of our twenty-five starters all the way to the end.

After the first series, as Jim Reid and I walked to the location of the second series, a field trial friend approached and ask how many dogs we had called back.

"All of them," I said.

"What! You're joking!" he answered. "Good grief, your next test is gonna have to be a real killer, isn't it?"

"Why?" I said.

"Well, if it isn't . . . " he started, but then he stopped, chuckled at his own misunderstanding of this new format, and added, "I see what you mean. Good luck!"

After each series, we called back every dog that had not committed some unpardonable offense, like breaking, switching, failing to find a mark, or going out of control on a blind. I'm not sure how many dogs ran all five series, but I'd guess it was about eighteen. Most of the dogs entered were well-trained field trial retrievers, so we saw lots of very good work.

Unfortunately, I cannot remember the layout of any of the tests Jim Reid and I ran in the master level. We did, of course, run the mandatory upland quartering and tracking tests. We also ran blind retrieves on land

and in water. But all of our marks were doubles. Jim and I agreed ahead of time to run no triples, primarily because back then many retriever-owning hunters (rightly or wrongly) felt that triples smacked too much of field trials, not of actual hunting. Besides, the rules required only multiple marks, and we felt we could set up doubles that would prove whether a dog could mark. We didn't need triples. For some time thereafter, when judging, I continued to limit master level marks to doubles, but eventually triples became a requirement.

The original AKC judge's sheet had eleven categories, instead of today's five, each to be graded numerically (0 to 10) for each of the five series. That makes a total of fifty-five possible numbers to be figured into each dog's final score. And, as I said, we carried about eighteen dogs all the way, so we ended up with lots of numbers to crunch. After the last series, Jim Reid, two volunteer assistants, and I spent ninety minutes doing arithmetic with an assortment of hand calculators just to determine which dogs had qualified! Thanks to the generosity of a kind club member, we did this around a table in an air-conditioned motor home. Outside, a sunburned and sweating group of handlers waited with justified impatience for the results. Some of them had traveled quite a distance to run this inaugural event and wanted to start back toward home as early as possible. I don't recall exactly how many dogs passed, but I would guess it was about twelve or fourteen.

Happily, after using that eleven-category judging form for a year or so, AKC streamlined it down to today's five categories. It also dropped the upland quartering and tracking tests.

🐾 I'm So Glad I Was There!

From these perhaps awkward beginnings, our hunt test programs have grown in size, frequency, and sophistication to become the truly wonderful sport they are today. I enjoy them now, and I'm glad I've been able to watch them grow and change over the years, but most of all I'm so glad I didn't miss out on their beginnings back in the early 1980s. If you weren't there, I hope these few recollections can give you a little of the flavor of the early days of these wonderful programs. Enjoy!

✎ Canada

In 1996, the Canadian Kennel Club (CKC) initiated a hunting test program quite similar to that of AKC. It has the same three graduated testing levels, with the same three names (junior, senior, master), and the same three titles (JH, SH, MH). The CKC senior and master levels include upland hunting tests. CKC offers an additional title, Grand Master Hunter (GMH), for dogs that qualify in the master level ten additional times after completing the MH title.

In 1987, CKC initiated a working certificate program similar to those of our various national breed clubs. This CKC program has three graduated levels, each with its own title: Working Certificate (WC), Working Certificate Intermediate (WCI), and Working Certificate Excellent (WCX). The work required at each level is similar to, but less difficult than, that of the corresponding hunting test level. To earn a title, the dog must qualify only once, whereas in the hunting test program the dog must qualify multiple times for each title. Like the various national breed club working certificate tests, the CKC working certificate program is designed primarily for conformation breeders who want to prove their stock in the field without getting too deeply involved. Because CKC, the major Canadian registry, sponsors this program, the titles go into certified pedigrees and so carry much more weight among breeders than do the similar titles offered by national breed clubs. Perhaps AKC and UKC should emulate this CKC working certificate program.

✎ An Auxiliary UKC/HRC Program

In 1999, UKC/HRC inaugurated their "upland hunts" to demonstrate the ability of retrievers to hunt upland game birds in a manner we normally associate with spaniels. This is a single-level program, in which a dog can earn the Upland Hunter (UH) title by qualifying in four upland hunts. Each upland hunt has three series: a walk-up, a quartering test, and a tracking test. In the walk-up, the dog must walk along at heel, sit when a bird flushes, remain steady to wing and shot, and retrieve on command. In the quartering test, the dog must hunt an area systematically while remaining within gun range, flush a bird, sit, remain steady to wing and shot, and then retrieve on command. In the tracking test, the dog must trail a simulated "runner" for between forty and seventy-five yards.

This is an auxiliary program for those who hunt upland birds as well as waterfowl with their retrievers. Since, unlike the other hunt test formats, it is a single-level program, it will be treated separately throughout this book.

Chapter 3
Hunt Test Popularity

REGULAR HUNT TESTS

By "regular hunt tests," I mean the multilevel, non-slip retriever formats implemented by AKC, UKC/HRC, and NAHRA in the mid-1980s and by CKC in 1996. This term doesn't include the more specialized single-level UKC/HRC upland hunts implemented in 1999, which are covered separately at the end of this chapter.

Those of us who have been involved from their beginnings in late 1983 have watched the exploding—almost exponential—growth of these hunt tests with something approaching disbelief. Certainly nothing in the world of dog games has even approached it. Unfortunately, I didn't start tracking statistics on this growth until 1994, after the initial explosion was over. However, I have maintained data on every year between 1994 and 2003, so I can at least show the growth that took place during what we might call the "second decade." Unfortunately, my statistics are limited to the AKC, UKC/HRC, and NAHRA formats. I didn't keep similar statistics for the CKC format (*mea culpa*) and CKC was unable to provide them for this book.

We can measure growth in three ways: the total number of events per year, the total number of starters per year, and the average number of starters per event per year. Since the sponsoring organizations (AKC, UKC/HRC, and NAHRA) limit the number of events each club may conduct per year, growth in total number of events means that hunt test enthusiasts are forming more clubs to conduct hunt tests. Since the nature of a retriever's work tends to limit each owner to one or two dogs, growth in total number of starters means that more people are buying retrievers and entering their retrievers in hunt tests. Growth in average starters per event means that the growth in starters exceeds the growth in events,

CHART 1
NUMBER OF EVENTS: 1994–2003

TYPE / LEVEL	1994	1995	1996	1997	1998	1999	2000	2001	2002	2003	Average
AKC HUNTING TESTS											
Junior	223	233	248	255	238	267	271	304	287	325	265
Senior	215	215	232	236	217	236	238	261	242	275	237
Master	186	197	212	216	196	215	202	221	203	214	206
Total (1)	**223**	**237**	**252**	**258**	**240**	**269**	**272**	**305**	**291**	**326**	**267**
HRC/UKC HUNTS											
Started	132	146	143	155	177	178	204	223	208	223	179
Seasoned	132	146	143	155	176	178	203	221	208	223	179
Finished	130	146	143	155	177	179	206	220	211	224	179
Total (1)	**132**	**146**	**143**	**155**	**177**	**180**	**206**	**223**	**211**	**224**	**180**
NAHRA FIELD TESTS											
Started	162	157	158	164	148	160	170	158	124	109	151
Intermediate	160	152	152	162	144	152	159	159	118	108	147
Senior	139	138	145	154	132	143	153	141	116	100	136
Total (1)	**166**	**170**	**170**	**187**	**160**	**172**	**183**	**173**	**135**	**115**	**163**
TOTALS FOR ALL PROGRAMS											
Lowest level	517	536	549	574	563	605	645	685	619	657	595
Middle level	507	513	527	553	537	566	600	641	568	606	563
Highest level	455	481	500	525	505	537	561	582	530	538	521
Total of Totals (1)	**521**	**553**	**565**	**600**	**577**	**621**	**661**	**701**	**637**	**665**	**610**
UKC/HRC UPLAND HUNTS											
Total (2)	—	—	—	—	—	**31**	**29**	**40**	**58**	**67**	**45**

Nota bene:
1. Since some events have only one or two testing levels, the total number of events
   can exceed the total number for any one testing level.
2. UKC/HRC Upland Hunts, which started in 1999, have only one testing level.

Hunt tests appeal to a wide variety of people, and as this group shows, success is possible for all who train their retrievers well.

which in turn suggests that the number of clubs will continue to increase.

Chart 1 shows the number of events at each level of each format for each year between 1994 and 2003. Chart 2 shows the number of starters at each level of each format for those years. Chart 3 shows the average number of starters at each level of each format for those years. These charts show the actual numbers. However, since the three formats differ widely in overall popularity, it's easier to compare their growth by using percentages. Therefore, the following analyses will rely mostly on percentages rather than actual numbers.

↳ Number of Events

As stated above, Chart 1 shows the annual numbers of events for each level within each hunt test format. Since many events have only one or two levels, the total events for each year may not be the same as that for any of the three levels, and in fact can exceed the total for any of the three levels. For the same reason, in each program, total growth for ten years can exceed the growth of any of its testing levels. Chart 1 also shows the annual totals for the combined levels of all formats. Then, at the very bottom, it shows the annual total events for UKC/HRC upland hunts, which are single-level quartering and flushing tests introduced in 1999. This program isn't included in the overall totals for a couple of reasons: First, it differs in nature from the three retriever testing formats; and second, it has only one level.

In the AKC hunting test format, the number of lowest level (junior) events grew by 45.7%, the middle level (senior) by 27.9%, and the highest level (master) by 15.1%. Overall, AKC events grew by 46.2%. In 1994, when there were 223 AKC events, if they were evenly distributed through the year, there would have been 4.3 events every weekend. However, we know they aren't evenly distributed throughout the year. Very few events are held in December, January, and February. If we eliminate those thirteen weekends, we can estimate that there were 5.7 events every weekend. In 2003, when there were 326 events, there would have been an average of 6.3 events per weekend in a twelve-month year, or 8.4 events in the more realistic nine-month year. AKC won't allow two clubs within about 200 miles of each other to hold hunt tests on the same weekend, so those 8.4 events were necessarily scattered across the country. Actually, most hunt tests are conducted between April and September, so they're especially dense nationwide during those peak months. This, of course, means that if you want to run your pooch in AKC hunt tests, you probably won't have to travel very far to do so.

In the UKC/HRC hunt format, the number of lowest level (started) events grew by 68.9%, the middle level (seasoned) by 68.9%, and the highest level (finished) by 72.3%. Overall, UKC/HRC events grew by 69.7%. In 1994, when there were 132 UKC/HRC events, if we figure weekend averages using the twelve-month year, there were 2.5 events per weekend. If we use the nine-month year, there were 3.4. In 2003, when there were 224 events, the twelve-month year would have averaged 4.3 events per weekend, and the nine-month year would have averaged 5.7 per weekend. UKC also controls the distance between "competing" events, so these events would have been well scattered. Since most events fall between April and September, you wouldn't have to travel far during that peak season to find a UKC/HRC event.

In the NAHRA field test format, total events peaked in 2000 and declined thereafter. Between 1994 and 2000, the number of lowest level (started) events grew by 4.9%, while the middle level (intermediate) declined by 0.6%, and the highest level (senior) grew by 10.1%. But then between 2000 and 2003, the lowest level declined by 35.9%, the middle level declined by 32.1%, and the highest level declined by 34.6%. Thus, overall—that is, between 1994 and 2003—the lowest level declined by 32.7%, the middle level declined by 32.5%, and the highest level declined by 28.1%. Overall, NAHRA events declined by 37.2%. In 2003, if we figure using a twelve-month year, there were only 2.2 NAHRA events per weekend. If we use the nine-month year, there were 2.9. Thus, NAHRA events have become pretty widely scattered since 2000.

Even with the dramatic decline in NAHRA events, the totals for all formats combined show healthy growth. The combined lowest levels grew by 27.1%, the combined middle levels grew by 19.5%, the combined highest levels grew by 18.2%, and the combined total events grew by 27.6%. In 1994, figuring with a twelve-month calendar, there were an average of 10.0 hunt tests per weekend nationwide. Figuring with a nine-month calendar, there were an average of 13.4. In 2003, those numbers had grown to 12.8 and 17.1. Thus, between 1994 and 2003 the average number of hunt tests grew by three or four per weekend!

⤷Number of Starters

Chart 2 shows the annual numbers of starters for each testing level within each format. It also shows the annual totals for each testing level of all three formats combined. At the very bottom, it shows the annual numbers of starters for UCK/HRC upland hunts.

In the AKC hunting test format, the number of starters in lowest level (junior) events grew by 54.5%, the middle level (senior) by 101.7%, and the highest level (master) by 95.7%. Overall, AKC starters grew by 78.7%.

In the UKC/HRC hunt format, the number of starters in lowest level (started) events grew by 124.5%, the middle level (seasoned) by 94.3%, and the highest level (finished) by 169.3%. Overall, UKC/HRC starters grew by 133.9%

In the NAHRA field test format, the number of starters peaked in 2000 and declined thereafter. Between 1994 and 2000, the lowest level (started) grew by 33.6%, the middle level (intermediate) grew by 1.1%, while the highest level (senior) declined by 0.1%. But then between 2000 and 2003, the lowest level declined by 41.0%, the middle level declined by 44.0%, and the highest level declined by 46.0%.

CHART 2

NUMBER OF STARTERS: 1994–2003

TYPE / LEVEL	1994	1995	1996	1997	1998	1999	2000	2001	2002	2003	Average
AKC HUNTING TESTS											
Junior	8,535	9,490	10,652	10,960	10,603	11,663	12,301	12,748	12,849	13,187	11,299
Senior	4,394	4,632	5,138	5,960	5,567	6,565	7,198	7,837	8,393	8,863	6,455
Master	6,175	6,964	8,020	8,320	8,413	10,535	10,048	11,041	12,233	12,082	9,383
Total	**19,104**	**21,086**	**23,810**	**25,240**	**24,583**	**28,763**	**29,547**	**31,626**	**33,475**	**34,132**	**27,137**
UKC/HRC HUNTS											
Started	2,320	2,440	2,496	2,940	3,077	2,867	3,379	4,704	4,910	5,209	3,434
Seasoned	2,517	2,851	2,821	3,383	3,827	3,650	4,248	4,491	4,389	4,890	3,707
Finished	3,432	4,178	4,358	5,382	6,607	6,843	7,414	7,512	8,458	9,241	6,343
Total	**8,269**	**9,469**	**9,675**	**11,705**	**13,511**	**13,360**	**15,041**	**16,707**	**17,757**	**19,340**	**13,484**
NAHRA FIELD TESTS											
Started	2,347	2,764	2,643	3,229	2,881	2,873	3,136	2,666	2,192	1,852	2,658
Intermediate	1,779	1,615	1,691	1,879	1,602	1,755	1,798	1,512	1,179	1,007	1,582
Senior	2,605	2,451	2,311	2,827	2,353	2,767	2,582	2,149	1,554	1,393	2,299
Total	**6,731**	**6,830**	**6,645**	**7,935**	**6,836**	**7,395**	**7,516**	**6,327**	**4,925**	**4,252**	**6,539**
TOTALS FOR ALL PROGRAMS											
Lowest level	13,202	14,694	15,791	17,129	16,561	17,403	18,816	20,118	19,951	20,248	17,391
Middle level	8,690	9,098	9,650	11,222	10,996	11,970	13,244	13,840	13,961	14,460	11,713
Highest level	12,212	13,593	14,689	16,529	17,373	20,145	20,044	20,702	22,245	22,716	18,025
Total	**34,104**	**37,385**	**40,130**	**44,880**	**44,930**	**49,518**	**52,104**	**54,660**	**56,157**	**57,724**	**47,160**
UKC/HRC UPLAND HUNTS											
	---	---	---	---	---	**518**	**487**	**627**	**944**	**1,005**	**716**

Nota bene: UKC/HRC Upland Hunts, which started in 1999, have only one testing level.

Thus, overall—that is, between 1994 and 2003—the lowest level declined by 21.1%, the middle level declined by 43.4%, and the highest level declined by 46.5%. Overall, NAHRA starters declined by 36.8%.

Here, too, in spite of the dramatic decline in NAHRA starters, the totals for all formats combined show healthy growth. The combined lowest levels grew by 53.4%, the combined middle levels grew by 66.4%, the combined highest levels grew by 86.0%, and the combined total starters grew by 69.3%.

Average Starters/Event

Chart 3 shows the annual average numbers of starters per event for each testing level within each format. It also shows the annual totals for starters per event for each testing level of all three formats combined. At the very bottom, it shows the annual average numbers of starters for UCK/HRC upland hunts.

In the AKC hunting test format, the average starters per event in lowest level (junior) events grew by 7.9%, the middle level (senior) grew by 60.0%, and the highest level (master) grew by 72.7%. Overall, AKC average starters grew by 22.1%. Such growth means that, at each level, the total number of starters grew substantially faster than the number of events. Of course, Charts 1 and 2 show that this is precisely what has happened. Even though total events grew at an amazing rate, total starters went through the roof.

In the UKC/HRC hunt format, the average starters per lowest level (started) event grew by 27.8%, the middle level (seasoned) grew by 94.3%, and the highest level (finished) grew by 57.7%. Overall, UKC/HRC average starters grew by 36.5%.

In the NAHRA field test format, the average starters per event peaked in 1999 and declined thereafter. Between 1994 and 1999, the lowest level (started) grew by 20.0%, the middle level (intermediate) grew by 9.1%, while the highest level (senior) remained flat. But then between 1999 and 2003, the lowest level declined by 5.6%, the middle level declined by 25.0%, and the highest level declined by 26.3%. Overall—that is, between 1994 and 2003—the lowest level grew by 13.3%, the middle level declined by 18.2%, and the highest level

CHART 3

AVERAGE NUMBER OF STARTERS: 1994–2003

TYPE / LEVEL	1994	1995	1996	1997	1998	1999	2000	2001	2002	2003	Average
AKC HUNTING TESTS											
Junior	38	41	43	43	45	44	45	42	45	41	43
Senior	20	22	22	25	26	28	30	30	35	32	27
Master	33	35	38	39	43	49	50	50	60	57	45
Total (1)	**86**	**89**	**95**	**98**	**102**	**107**	**109**	**104**	**115**	**105**	**101**
UKC/HRC HUNTS											
Started	18	17	18	19	17	16	17	20	24	23	19
Seasoned	19	20	20	22	22	21	21	20	21	22	21
Finished	26	29	31	35	37	38	36	34	40	41	35
Total (1)	**63**	**65**	**68**	**76**	**76**	**74**	**73**	**75**	**84**	**86**	**74**
NAHRA FIELD TESTS											
Started	15	18	17	20	20	18	18	17	18	17	18
Intermediate	11	11	11	12	11	12	11	10	10	9	11
Senior	19	18	16	18	18	19	17	15	13	14	17
Total (1)	**41**	**40**	**39**	**42**	**43**	**43**	**41**	**37**	**37**	**37**	**40**
UKC/HRC UPLAND HUNTS (2)											
	---	---	---	---	---	17	17	16	16	15	16

Nota bene:
1. Since some events don't include all three testing levels, the total starters may not equal the sum of the entries for the three testing levels.
2. UKC/HRC Upland Hunts, which started in 1999, have only one testing level.

declined by 26.3%. NAHRA total average starters declined by 9.8%. This highest level plunge in all numbers (events, starters, and average starters) is especially significant, for at that level, NAHRA (like AKC and UKC/HRC) offers special incentives (annual invitational events and an additional, prestigious title) to induce people to continue running their titled dogs year after year. Thus this highest-level plunge indicates that NAHRA is not only failing to attract new people, but is even losing an alarming number of the old-time campaigners.

Unlike Charts 1 and 2, Chart 3 doesn't include averages for all three formats combined. Such numbers, although easily computed, wouldn't offer meaningful information in the sense that combined total events and combined total starters do. These latter two indicate the overall popularity of hunt tests. Combined average starters would add nothing to that. On the other hand, the average number of starters for each format does indicate the typical sizes of events in each format. The growth in those numbers indicates whether (and by what rate) the growth of total starters has exceeded the growth in total events.

ꝏ Conclusions

Across the board, UKC/HRC's program has outgrown AKC's. Granted, UKC/HRC started out with much lower numbers than AKC. Granted, also, even after its amazing growth for ten years, in 2003 UKC/HRC hunts still had much lower numbers in all three categories (events, starters, average starters) than AKC hunting tests. Nevertheless, the gap is closing.

The AKC hunting test program, which has always been the largest in every category, continues to grow at an extremely rapid rate. Someday it will level off, but that day may be many years in the future.

The NAHRA field test program appears to be in a life-threatening decline. Unless someone does something to turn this program around, the death rattle can't be many years down the road. Perhaps this illustrates the difficulty of sponsoring any dog activity without the support of a major dog registry. If that's the case, NAHRA's downfall began way back in 1984, shortly after that initial UKC/NAHRA hunt test in Louisiana, when NAHRA separated from UKC to form an alliance with

AKC, which alliance unraveled before June 1985 when AKC launched their own program of hunting tests.

On the brighter side, whatever losses NAHRA has suffered since 2000 have become gains for the other two programs. Judging from the numbers in Charts 1, 2, and 3, those who abandoned NAHRA must have begun running in AKC and UKC/HRC events. In fact, the growth in these other two programs, and especially in the UKC/HRC program, indicates that they not only absorbed NAHRA's losses but also attracted many additional new people every year.

The Future

Like all statisticians, when I study numbers like those in Charts 1, 2, and 3, I feel an almost irresistible urge to make bold predictions about the future as a function of the data I have on the recent past. However, having been embarrassed quite often by the inaccuracy of my predictions, I have developed the caution necessary to resist that urge. Thus, I won't offer you a glowing picture of the future. I'll only state the obvious: If nothing untoward happens (World War III, another Great Depression, another bubonic plague, and so on), it appears that hunt test popularity will continue to grow for several more years before stabilizing at some very healthy level.

UKC/HRC UPLAND HUNTS

These hunts simulate hunting upland game birds on land and in cover, with a retriever performing work normally associated with flushing spaniels, namely, quartering, flushing, and retrieving. Retriever owners have long used their dogs most effectively in this manner. It was incorporated into the original AKC and NAHRA formats, but was later dropped from that of AKC. In 1999, UKC/HRC developed a separate program, with separate events and separate titles, for such work.

If growth in popularity is any indication (and it surely is!), this was an excellent idea. Chart 1 shows that the number of these events more than doubled in the five years between 1999 and 2003. Chart 2 shows that the number of starters has almost doubled in the same period. Chart 3 shows that the average number of starters has remained constant through this period. In other words, so far, the growth of starters has about matched that of events. Most of those who run their dogs in these events also run in regular hunt tests.

If these trends continue, these upland hunts will continue being a strong auxiliary program for retriever owners who use their dogs for upland hunting as well as for waterfowling.

Chapter 4
The Challenge of Hunt Tests

REGULAR HUNT TESTS

Here again, by "regular hunt tests," I mean the multilevel, non-slip retriever formats implemented by AKC, UKC/HRC, and NAHRA in the mid-1980s and by CKC in 1996. This term doesn't include the more specialized single-level UKC/HRC upland hunts implemented in 1999, which are covered separately at the end of this chapter.

Initial Hostility

People who were dissatisfied with field trials—in fact, disgruntled with field trials—developed hunt tests. Not surprisingly, most of the early participants were also people with similar anti–field-trial feelings. Thus, anti–field-trial rhetoric flooded the magazines devoted to hunt tests. Predictably, field trialers reacted with similar anti–hunt-test sentiments and rhetoric. Thus, considerable hostility sprang up immediately between hunt test "plebeians" and field trial "patricians." Those who developed hunt tests attacked the complexity and artificiality of field trials, even to the point of claiming that field trial dogs couldn't hunt. This is utter nonsense, of course, as many field trials dogs have proved to me and anyone else who has hunted with them. However, many early hunt test participants proclaimed this nonsense as gospel. For their part, field trialers belittled hunt tests, claiming that the titles were "cheap," awarded too easily because they involved no head-to-head competition with top dogs, as field trials do. They also claimed that, in the eyes of many, cheap hunt test titles would cheapen field trial titles. They feared that the general public, especially the puppy-buying public, would say, "Hey, we see so many dogs with so many titles. How can any of them mean anything?"

I might add that these hostilities and consequent word-wars between hunt testers and field trialers also took place in two other dog game areas: in 1986 when AKC introduced hunting tests for pointing breeds; and when AKC introduced hunting tests for flushing spaniels. I was there for all three beginnings, and was amazed at how similar the initial hostilities were between hunt testers and field trialers in each venue.

Happily, these hostilities have died down in all three venues (retrievers, pointing breeds, and flushing spaniels). In fact, in all three many people run their dogs in both hunt tests and field trials. Some judge both formats, which may not be an unmixed blessing, but it does help maintain the peace.

🦅 The Indictment

In all three venues, the major charge leveled by field trialers against the new hunt test programs was that the titles, not being competitive, would be so easy to earn that they would be meaningless.

🦅 The Case for the Defense

Now that hunt tests are twenty years old, we have sufficient data to prove that, although these titles (unlike competitive field trial titles) are achievable by any dog with proper breeding and training, they are (like noncompetitive obedience titles) quite challenging. Chart 4 shows the percent of starters qualifying at every level of the AKC, UKC/HRC, and NAHRA hunt test formats for the years from 1994 through 2003. I didn't keep similar statistics on the CKC format (*mea culpa*), and CKC was unable to provide them to me for this book.

To evaluate these percentages, we need a yardstick that indicates what these percentages should be in a sufficiently challenging program. The yardstick I use—that is, my estimate of a standard set of "proper" percentages—is as follows: At the lowest level, no more than 75% of the starters should qualify; at the middle level, no more than 60%; highest level, no more than 55%. (I'd lower the standard for the highest level to 50% if it weren't for the high percentage of titled dogs that continue to run at this level because of the special incentives

CHART 4

PERCENT OF STARTERS QUALIFYING
1994 - 2003

TYPE / LEVEL	1994	1995	1996	1997	1998	1999	2000	2001	2002	2003	Average
AKC HUNTING TESTS (1)											
Junior	63%	64%	66%	66%	69%	67%	68%	67%	66%	66%	66%
Senior	49%	52%	52%	52%	54%	51%	48%	52%	48%	49%	51%
Master	47%	47%	46%	47%	50%	47%	44%	44%	42%	42%	46%
UKC/HRC HUNTS (1)											
Started	75%	76%	51%	80%	80%	80%	82%	82%	83%	82%	77%
Seasoned	54%	53%	52%	57%	61%	62%	64%	63%	64%	64%	59%
Finished	52%	50%	49%	56%	57%	55%	56%	58%	55%	56%	54%
NAHRA FIELD TESTS (1)											
Started	63%	68%	69%	70%	72%	71%	70%	71%	75%	72%	70%
Intermediate	53%	51%	49%	54%	52%	52%	51%	48%	52%	52%	51%
Senior	55%	56%	53%	59%	55%	57%	58%	53%	55%	50%	55%
UKC/HRC UPLAND HUNTS (1 & 2)											
	---	---	---	---	---	66%	67%	65%	70%	66%	67%

Nota bene:
1. All percentages have been rounded to the nearest whole number.
2. UKC/HRC Upland Hunts, which started in 1999, have only one testing level.

offered by all three sponsoring organizations.) If you think my yard-stick too generous, apply it to our schools and colleges. If each year only 75% of grade school kids passed, only 60% of high schoolers advanced, and only 50% of college kids earned Ds or better, parents would be storming the schools, hanging teachers (at least in effigy), and demanding government action.

Nota bene 1: The average number of attempts required to earn a title offers another way to look at the challenge associated with that title. We can calculate the number of attempts the average dog requires to earn a specific title by dividing the number of qualifying scores required by the average qualifying percentage for that title.

Nota bene 2: Not every dog is average. Some dogs earn a given title in the minimum number of attempts, while others could run for-ever without ever earning even one qualifying score. Most dogs, whether ultimately successful or not, fall somewhere in between these extremes. For example, I once washed out a Golden that failed in four out of five attempts in the AKC junior level. At that rate, to title him, I'd have had to run him in twenty events. Thanks a lot, but no thanks. Nevertheless, the above-computed average number of attempts required for each title does indicate how demanding the judging standard for that format and level is.

Now with all that in mind, let's look at each level of each program, level by level.

The Lowest Level

In each program, the lowest level exists primarily to break in new people and new dogs. The work is quite basic, intended more to encourage further training and participation than to challenge and frustrate them. After all, no one gets rich from stud fees for a dog titled only at this lowest level.

In the AKC junior level, the overall average qualifying percent for the ten years is 66%. The lowest annual percentage was 63% (in 1994). The highest was 69% (in 1998). In the lowest year, it took an average of 6.3 attempts for a dog to qualify four times and earn the JH title. In the highest year, it took 5.8 attempts. In an average year, it took 6.1 attempts. Clearly, according to our yardstick, earning the AKC JH title is a significant challenge.

In the UKC/HRC started level, the overall average qualifying percent is 77%. The lowest annual percentage was an anomalous 51% (in 1996). The highest was 83% (in 2002). In the lowest year, it took an average of 7.8 attempts to qualify four times and thereby earn the SHR title. In the highest year, it took only 4.8 attempts. In an average year, it took 5.2 attempts. According to our yardstick, earning the SHR title is not quite as challenging as it should be, but not far off the mark overall.

In the NAHRA started level, the overall average qualifying percent 70%. The lowest annual percentage was 63% (in 1994). The highest was 75% (in 2002). In the lowest year, it took an average of 6.3 attempts to qualify four times and thereby earn the SR title. In the highest year, it took 5.3 attempts. In an average year, it took 5.7 attempts. Clearly, according to our yardstick, earning the SR title is adequately challenging.

Overall, according to our yardstick, earning a lowest level title is adequately challenging.

🐾 The Middle Level

The middle level requires work appropriate for a good day-in, day-out hunting retriever. The titles at this level have real meaning in pedigrees, whether one reads them for breeding or puppy-buying purposes. Therefore, we should expect the standard to be significantly higher at this level than at the lowest level.

In the AKC senior level, the overall average qualifying percent is 51%. The lowest annual percentage was 48% (in 2000 and 2002). The highest was 54% (in 1998). Earning the SH title requires four qualifying scores for a dog with the JH title, and five for a dog without that title. Therefore, in the lowest year, a JH-titled dog required an average of 8.3 attempts to earn the SH title. In the highest year, such a dog required an average of 7.4 attempts. In an average year, such a dog required an average of 7.8 attempts. Similarly, in the lowest year, a non-JH-titled dog required an average of 10.4 attempts. In the highest year, such a dog required an average of 9.3 attempts. In an average year, such a dog required an average of 9.8 attempts. According to our yardstick, then, earning the SH title is extremely challenging.

In the UKC/HRC seasoned level, the overall average qualifying percent is 59%. The lowest annual percentage was 52% (in 1996). The highest was 64% (in 2000, 2002, and 2003). Earning the HR title requires three qualifying scores for the dog with the SHR title and four for a dog without that title. Therefore, in the lowest year, an SHR-titled dog required 5.8 attempts. In the highest year, such a dog required 4.7 attempts. In an average year, such a dog required 5.1 attempts. Similarly, in the lowest year, a non-SHR-titled dog required 7.7 attempts. In the highest year, such a dog required 6.3 attempts. In an average year, such a dog required 6.8 attempts. Although the average percent (59%) approximates our yardstick, the trend at this level of the UKC/HRC program since 2000 has been upward, with the qualifying percentages significantly higher than our yardstick.

In the NAHRA intermediate level, the overall average qualifying percentage is 51%. The lowest annual percentage was 48% (in 2001). The

This female Lab, "Smokey" (Blackstar's Smart Smoke, MH, MNH, HOF, QAA) has met and mastered the challenge of AKC hunt tests. She first earned her AKC Master Hunter (MH) title. Then she earned her Master National Hunter (MNH) title by qualifying in two AKC annual Master National Invitational Hunting Tests. She was enrolled in the Hall of Fame (HOF) after qualifying in her Third Master National. On the left is her trainer/handler, pro Lonny Taylor. On the right is her owner, Vicki DeMott.

highest was 54% (in 1997). Earning the WR title requires three qualifying scores for the dog with the SR title, and four for the dog without that title. Therefore, in the lowest year, an SR-titled dog required 6.3 attempts. In the highest year, such a dog required 5.6 attempts. In an average year, such a dog required 5.9 attempts. Similarly, in the lowest year, a non-SR-titled dog required 8.3 attempts. In the highest year, such a dog required 7.4 attempts. In an average year, such a dog required 7.8 attempts. Clearly, according to our yardstick, earning the WR title is extremely challenging.

Overall, according to our yardstick, the middle level is a mixed bag. The AKC and NAHRA programs offer extremely challenging middle levels, but the UKC/HRC program offers one that has become somewhat less than adequately challenging in recent years.

🐾 The Highest Level

The work at this level should challenge even the best-bred and best-trained retriever. Any dog earning a title at this level should be in the "every hunter's dream dog" class. Therefore, the judging standard should be quite high. However, another factor comes into play at this level, in that, in each format, the sponsoring organization offers people powerful incentives to continue running their titled dogs year after year. These incentives are extra, high-prestige titles plus annual invitational tests. Since so many already titled dogs run at this level, we should expect the qualifying percentage to be higher than it would be if only untitled dogs were running.

In the AKC master level, the overall average qualifying percent is 46%. The lowest was 42% (in 2002 and 2003). The highest was 50% (in 1998). Earning the MH title requires five qualifying scores for a dog with the SH title, and six for the dog without that title. Therefore, in the lowest year, an SH-titled dog required an average of 11.9 attempts to earn the MH title. In the highest year, such a dog required 10.0 attempts. In an average year, such a dog required 10.9 attempts. Similarly, in the lowest year, a non-SH-titled dog required an average of 14.3 attempts. In the highest year, such a dog required 12.0 attempts. In an average year, such a dog required 13.0 attempts. Clearly, according to our yardstick, earning the MH title is so challenging that it borders on the unreasonable. The fact that the qualifying percent has been dropping steadily since 1998 is also rather alarming.

In the UKC/HRC finished level, the overall average qualifying percent is 54%. The lowest annual percentage was 49% (in 1996). The highest was 58% (in 2001). Since the HRCH title requires somewhere between six and ten qualifying scores, depending on whether the dog has the SHR and/or the HR titles, the average dog requires somewhere between 10.7 and 17.9 attempts to earn the HRCH title. Clearly, according to our yardstick, the HRCH title is adequately challenging.

In the NAHRA senior level, the overall average qualifying percent is 55%. The lowest annual percentage was 50% (in 2003). The highest was 59% (in 1997). Earning the MHR title requires four qualifying scores for the dog with the WR title, and five for the dog without that title. Therefore, in the lowest year, a WR-titled dog required 8.0 attempts to earn the MHR title. In the highest year, such a dog required 6.8 attempts. In an average year, such a dog required 7.3 attempts. Similarly, in the lowest year, a non-WR-titled dog required 10.0 attempts to earn the MHR title. In the highest year, such a dog required 8.5 attempts. In an average year, such a dog required 9.1 attempts. According to our yardstick, this program is adequately challenging.

Overall, according to our yardstick, the highest level offers titles that vary in challenge from adequate (on the button with our yardstick) to bordering on unreasonably difficult.

The Verdict

Hunt tests overall have clearly been proven innocent of the charge that they award cheap titles to unworthy dogs. Although in hunt tests dogs don't have to defeat other dogs to earn titles, the standards by which the judges make their decisions are sufficiently demanding to preclude any possibility of "cheap titles." Besides, from the very beginning, those who have judged hunt tests have been determined to make the titles highly meaningful. If anything, they have been too tough more often than too lenient, as almost any participant will testify. This has surprised no one who was familiar with obedience trials, in which titles are noncompetitively earned but extremely challenging.

UKC/HRC UPLAND HUNTS

Happily, this format made its debut after the hostility between field trialers and hunt testers had mostly died down. Of course, since this format has little or nothing in common with field trials, it didn't threaten field trialers in any way. Thus, no charge of "cheap titles" has ever been levied against this program.

What yardstick should we use to defend the program against this nonexistent charge? Although it seems silly to even bother, nevertheless, for consistency's sake, I'll toss out a number that seems reasonable to me: The qualifying percentage should be no higher than 65%.

Chart 4 shows that the overall average qualifying percentage is 67%. The lowest annual percentage was 65% (in 2001). The highest was 70% (in 2002). Since it takes four passes to earn the Upland Hunter (UH) title, in the lowest year, it took an average of 6.2 attempts to earn the title. In the highest year, it took 5.7 attempts. In an average year, it took 6.0. According to my admittedly arbitrary and perhaps indefensible yardstick, this program is not quite as challenging as it should be, but it's close enough to be worthwhile.

SECTION II

Successful Handling

Chapter 5
General Preparations

Okay, so you've decided to run your retriever in hunt tests. Perhaps when you bought your puppy, the breeder recommended this to you. Perhaps you bought a started or fully trained retriever for hunting and the seller recommended hunt tests. Perhaps you've been hunting with your retriever for years and have now decided to devote the long off-season to hunt tests. Perhaps you're a field trialer who wants to add this newer noncompetitive game to your recreational repertoire. Perhaps you ran retriever hunt tests several years ago, but stopped after Ol' Mallard-Muncher died, and you've recently brought a puppy and want to bring yourself up to date on the game. Perhaps you're a retriever-owning obedience trialer who has become fascinated by the training complexities of field work. Perhaps. Perhaps. Perhaps.

Whatever your situation, whatever your motivation, let's start at the beginning, that is, the point in time when you made this decision, for that's when you should begin preparing both yourself and your retriever for this wonderful off-season pastime. In this chapter you'll learn what you need to do, regardless of which hunt test format you prefer. (Incidentally, you don't have to choose one and exclude the others. You can run the same dog in all four formats if you so choose.)

LONG-RANGE PREPARATIONS

Join a Training Group

As soon as you decide to run in hunt tests, you should join a small group of people with similar goals who train together regularly. The

51

person from whom you bought your puppy or grown dog may be able to direct you to such a group. If not, go to the website (see the Appendix) of the organization that sponsors your chosen format (AKC, UKC/HRC, NAHRA, or CKC), where you'll find their affiliated clubs listed. Contact the club nearest your home and inquire about membership. Once you belong to such a club, finding a training group from among the members should be fairly easy. If you haven't decided on a format yet, go to all four websites and identify and contact nearby clubs. After talking to members of these clubs, you should be able to decide which format suits you best.

By joining a training group, you have several advantages not available to the solo retriever trainer. First, you'll gain access to whatever training grounds they use. Second, you'll gain mentors to guide you through the early stages of training. Third, you'll gain the helpers you need to be able to train your retrievers, since training-group members take turns throwing marks, planting blinds, acting as judges, and so forth, for one another. Finally, a training group works their dogs regularly, normally several times a week, which will motivate you to go out and train even when you don't feel like it.

With all the electronic gadgets available today, especially the very handy remote dummy and bird launchers, a person can train alone successfully to a far greater extent than was possible years ago. However, even today, no one can train a retriever well enough to succeed in any level of any hunt test format without human assistants, at least part of the time. Thus, you need to join a training group as soon as possible.

Know the Game

Whatever the game...poker, badminton, baseball, Monopoly...to be successful, you must know the rules. Not surprisingly then, without a thorough knowledge of hunt test rules, you will bomb out test after test (which can be as expensive as losing at poker night after night).

If you plan to run in AKC hunting tests for retrievers, you need a current copy of the AKC rule book. More than that, you need to read it, and reread it, and reread it, until you're completely familiar with at least those parts that apply to the level you intend to enter. Ditto for

UKC/HRC hunts, NAHRA field tests, and CKC hunt tests. Granted, reading any of these rule books is about as exciting as reading the manual that came with your washer or dryer. But you need the information, so drink some coffee and wade through the appropriate rule book, again and again and again. Then, periodically thereafter, grit your teeth and plow through it again. If you do, you'll receive no unpleasant surprises (that are legal) when you run your retriever in your chosen flavor of hunt tests.

If you have an opportunity to attend a seminar conducted by the appropriate sponsoring organization (AKC, UKC/HRC, NAHRA, or CKC) before entering your first test, by all means do so. You'll learn so much, and you'll be able to ask questions of authoritative experts. In fact, even after you've become an old hand at hunt tests, you shouldn't pass up these seminars. No one knows it all; you should try to learn more at every reasonable opportunity.

MID-RANGE PREPARATIONS

Let's say that you have been training with a group for quite a while, have read the rule book several times, and now feel your dog is nearly ready for his first real hunt test "experience." What should you do to facilitate success, between now and the time when you send in your first entry form?

Prepare Your Retriever

We call these events "hunt tests," and everyone involved tries mightily to make them as much like actual hunting as possible. However, they necessarily differ from hunting in many ways, and in every case, hunt tests are the more challenging of the two.

First off, the general environment at a hunt test presents both you and your dog with far more distractions, and far more disturbing distractions, than you'll encounter in the marshes and meadows: visual distractions, aural distractions and, for the dog, scent distractions. People and dogs are everywhere. People's voices sound everywhere, sometimes speaking, sometimes shouting, and sometimes blaring over a loud speaker. Dogs are barking. Cars and trucks are moving about. Occasionally a horn honks. Dead birds hang in a drying rack behind the judges. And so on. Thus, in training sessions, you should *frequently* simulate these conditions as best you and your training group can.

At hunt tests, you and your dog normally must wait in a holding blind while the dog ahead of you runs. Sometimes, especially if the actual test is a long way from the parking area, you may have to play work-up through a series of holding blinds before getting to the line. Thus, all through your training program, you need to accustom your dog to long waits in holding blinds, even when he's excited because he knows he's about to get to retrieve birds. You should buy or make a suitable holding blind and use it in training. Ideally, two or three people in your training group should have holding blinds, so you can set up a series of them, at least occasionally. In training, heel your dog on lead into the holding blind, have him sit, and wait...and wait. Whenever he gets antsy, give him a leash correction, and say, "No! Sit!" After he's comfortable with this, begin leaving him in the holding blind (on the command "Stay") while you walk away, at first staying within sight, but eventually going out of sight for at least a few seconds. If your dog will sit there quietly while you're out of sight, he has pretty well mastered the holding blind problem. Nevertheless, to avoid backsliding, use these blinds in training quite often.

While training, wear the same clothing you'll wear at hunt tests. This matters especially in the upper two levels of each format, which include blind retrieves. If, for example, in training you wear a long-sleeved white shirt while handling your dog on blind retrieves and then you switch to a camo shirt for the hunt test, you'll totally confuse him. Similarly, you should use the same whistles at a hunt test that you use in training. If you switch to, say, a louder whistle "just to make sure Ol' Plugged Ears hears me," he may hear the whistle all right, but ignore it because he doesn't realize you're the one blowing it.

Finally, you should realize that, at each level in each format, the typical test in hunt tests is significantly more difficult than a typical hunting retrieve. Hunt tests are intended to identify and reward the truly good hunting dogs, not the mediocrities, so the tests necessarily fall on the high end of the level of difficulty curve. Since this is a handling book, not a training book, it doesn't contain test setups as such.

Nevertheless, you need to know what "factors" (aka "hazards") can complicate the various tests and, knowing all this, you should prepare your dog in training sessions for the more difficult situations. (My book *Retriever Training Tests*, available through the publisher of this book, contains extensive test design information.)

Prepare Yourself

In training, you should establish a definite pace for your handling, one that's comfortable for both you and your dog. This is important in all handling situations, but especially in blind retrieves. At hunt tests, no matter how nervous and excited you may be, maintain that pace. Don't allow yourself to panic and freeze. Conversely, don't speed up. Either way, you'll confuse your dog.

Pro-golfing great Julius Boros was the calmest of competitors under pressure. Nothing ruffled him. Nothing hurried him. Nothing slowed him down. He played every shot as relaxed as if he were on the practice tee, not in a real tournament with thousands of dollars at stake on every stroke. When asked how he remained so calm, he answered offhandedly, "It's not your life and it's not your wife. It's just a game!" If you can tell yourself that while handling your retriever in hunt tests, you'll be much less apt to become excited and destroy the timing to which you've accustomed your dog.

In training, you should condition yourself to send your dog only after hearing someone acting as a judge call your number. In a hunt test, if you send him before the judge calls your number, your dog will be charged with a break and eliminated. Very frequently in training, you should have someone (even a noninvolved family member) act as judge and call your number. Also, remember that you don't have to send your dog immediately after hearing your number. Always look at his head first to make sure he's properly locked in before launching him on his hard-charging way.

Hunt Test Simulations

Before actually entering a hunt test, you and your training group should conduct several simulations to make sure all handlers and their dogs really are ready. Make these sessions as formal as possible, as much like an actual hunt test as you can. Ideally, you should go to a location you've never used before in training. If possible, every member of your group should bring his entire family, to simulate the crowd at a hunt test. You should set up holding blinds and a realistic line environment, with judges, their chairs, a drying rack with dead birds on it, many decoys, various game calls, lots of shooting, and so on. Play radios, tapes, or CDs near the line to simulate the noise level at a hunt test. Each member of your group should take his turn running his dog as he would in a hunt test. He should go through a series of holding blinds, send his dog only after the judge calls his number, hand each delivered bird to a judge, and heel his dog away from the line when he's finished.

One very important point: If you normally train with an e-collar, remove it for these simulations. If your dog goofs up, correct him in one of the old fashioned (before the e-collar) ways. In fact, you should hope your dog does indeed goof up so you can correct him. At a real hunt test, where he can't wear an e-collar, you can't correct him. Thus, if he goofs up at a hunt test and goes unpunished, especially several times, he will almost certainly become both "collar-wise" and "test-wise," which means that he'll have figured out that he can get away with things when he isn't wearing his e-collar (and therefore when he's at a hunt test) that he can't get away with in training. If, during these simulation sessions, you remove the e-collar and correct his errors in some other way, he's unlikely to figure out that you can't do the same at a hunt test. If you have these simulation sessions reasonably often, and if you do correct him by means other than the e-collar, he's unlikely to become either collar-wise or test-wise.

Spectate

Above all, before entering your first hunt test, you should attend a few of them, paying special attention to the level you intend to enter. What you see there will give you a fresh feel for the hunt test environment, an understanding of hunt test procedures, and some inkling of the type of tests you might expect when you enter your first one. And, of course, refreshing your knowledge of the rules immediately before

To learn about hunt tests, you need a knowledgeable mentor. Here pro trainer Lonny Taylor mentors Vicki DeMott at a hunt test, while Kathie Sinclair waits her turn to run in the holding blind.

spectating at real hunt tests will help you interpret what you see there.

Find a Mentor

You should ask an experienced person, perhaps someone from your training group, to accompany you and help you understand what you're watching. He can explain the challenges of each test, especially the hazards. He can explain what the judges are looking for in each test. He can also point out the virtues and vices of each dog/handler team running. Of course, you and he should converse thusly only when you are alone, with no one else within earshot. If, while standing near a stranger, either of you should make a negative comment about a test, a handler, or a dog, you can bet that said stranger is related to one of the judges or the handler involved. If Murphy had been a hunt tester, he would have made a law about this.

Come Early

You should arrive early enough to hear the judges' instructions to the handlers before the first test. Listen attentively not only to the judges' instructions but also to any handlers' questions and the judges' answers. Since you aren't actually running a dog, you should politely refrain from asking questions, especially any that may sound as if you were challenging the judges' knowledge of the rules. (Don't laugh, for

To train and prepare your retriever for hunt tests, you need to join a training group made up of other people with those same goals in mind. Here a training group prepares to set up a test during a training session.

overly enthusiastic spectators sometimes do such things!) In each succeeding test, arrive at the scene early enough to listen to the judges' instructions and so forth. If you don't understand something you hear, discuss the matter with your mentor who is accompanying you.

Watch each dog run. Actually, you'll learn more about the tests from the dogs that fail or do poorly than from the really good workers. Poor work normally indicates that the dog has failed to deal properly with one or more hazards. Thus, you'll learn to identify hazards more clearly from such dogs. If you're unclear about the hazards, ask your learned mentor-friend to point them out and explain them to you.

Watch each handler. Pay special attention to those whose dogs do excellent work. Notice how they help their dogs through quiet, subtle handling techniques. On the other hand, pay little attention to showboat handlers. Keep in mind that the handler goes to the line to help his dog retrieve the birds, not to audition for a part in a play or ballet, and certainly not to entertain the judges and gallery. Like good coaches in a football or basketball game, truly good, truly effective handlers are almost invisible, especially to the neophyte, who will notice only their dogs, not the handlers themselves. Ask your mentor to point out the good handlers and explain what they do and don't do that makes them so effective.

Mind Your Manners

No matter how well or poorly a dog may have done, you shouldn't comment to the handler as he leaves the line. His dog may have been dropped for a fault that you missed entirely, such as hardmouth. He may be frustrated and angry. If you rush up to him, smile broadly, and say, "Great job," he will almost certainly think you're being sarcastic. Even if his dog did fantastically well and he's ecstatically happy as he leaves the line, he'll enjoy the moment just as much without your congratulations. Of course, if you see smoke coming from his ears and fire in his eyes, you should let him work off his frustration in his own way. Most of all, if his dog did only so-so, he doesn't need your evaluation of what went wrong, believe me. If you have any suggestions "that might help the handler in the future," save them for your own future. Unfortunately, at hunt tests, as in so many other activities, it is the least knowledgeable persons who most frequently offer unsolicited advice. Frankly, most people who make a habit of offering unsolicited advice do so more to show off their supposedly superior knowledge than to help solve someone else's problems. Thus, I have a saying: *Unsolicited advice is usually worth far less than you pay for it.* As a given handler leaves the line, if you have any questions or comments about his dog's work, share them with your mentor, not the handler.

When you spectate at these initial hunt tests, in each series you'll see some dogs fail, and others do barely acceptable work. You may decide that your own beastie could certainly do better than many, perhaps even most, of the dogs entered. And maybe he could. Who knows? But, frankly, who cares? In the future, you'll have every opportunity to show everyone at hunt tests what a wonderful animal you have and what a great job you've done in training him. *So, don't bother telling anyone now, and especially don't tell anyone whose dog is doing poorly.* Every experienced handler has heard so many neophytes boast about how their un-entered super-dogs would tear up every test that their eyes tend to glass over at the approach of a new-comer. Thus, even the kindliest of them has taken secret delight when, at a later test, the bragging neophyte's dog bombs out in the first series without getting near the first bird. This happens all the time. If your dog is everything you think he is, he'll show everyone later when you actually run him in his first hunt test, so why bother telling anyone about his talents before then?

Stay Late

Stick around after the last test to witness the awarding of rosettes to the successful handlers. Watching this little ceremony will motivate you to train harder and get your dog truly ready for his first hunt test. As the marshal passes out the rosettes, and on into the evening, you'll hear a lot of talk among handlers about the tests, about their dogs, about their plans to correct problems. Here again, listen a lot and speak as little as possible. As a beginner, you're there to learn, and beginners learn far more while listening than while talking.

Of course, you should feel free to ask questions, as long as they are really questions and not challenges or lead-ins to stories about your own retriever's amazing talents. Listen to the answers, but realize that not all handlers are equally experienced, equally knowledgeable, equally eloquent. When different handlers offer conflicting answers to your questions, let your mentor help you sort them out. He knows training, he knows hunt tests, and he probably knows most of the handlers, so rely on him.

Analyze the Experience

As you drive home, let the events of the day run through your mind. Remember the various test setups. Analyze the hazards in each and how they affected the dogs' work. Reflect on the techniques of the good handlers, and let them sink into your subconscious. Recall the dogs' work: the excellent, the pretty good, the mediocre, the horrible...even the comical. Finally, picture the rosette the handler of each qualifying dog received at the end of the day: so large, with flowing ribbons, embossed with information about the event. Wouldn't such a rosette look nice in your den or office? Putting one (or more) of them there is entirely up to you.

✏Reread the Rule Book

At home, you should again reread the rule book for your chosen format. Having seen your first (or another) hunt test, you'll understand the rules more fully than you did before. If possible, after rereading the rule book, sit down with your mentor and go through them once again, asking him to explain anything on which you're still not clear.

✏Make Adjustments

As a result of spectating at a real hunt test, you may decide to refine your handling techniques to more closely approximate those of the successful handlers you've observed at these hunt tests. However, as explained above, you should choose your handling "models" most carefully, avoiding the showy, eye-catching exhibitionists. Above all, be consistent in your handling and give your dog plenty of time to get used to any changes you may decide to make.

Armed with all this additional information, you may also want to adjust your training program a bit here and there. Having seen several real hazards and how they can affect a dog's work quite negatively, you may decide your training tests have been too easy, too straightforward, too bland. If so, make such adjustments as your mentor agrees are appropriate for you and your dog.

SHORT-RANGE PREPARATIONS

✏Expert Opinion

Before sending in your first entry form, you should ask your mentor for his frank opinion as to whether both you and your retriever are truly ready for your first real hunt test. If he says yes, by all means send in your entry and prepare for the trip. If he says no, ask him what you still need to do to get ready, and then do it!

If you've run in one or more hunt tests, but without success, you should also seek your mentor's opinion before trying again. This may not only save you entry fees and travel expenses, but it also may prevent your dog from becoming test-wise.

🐾 Pre-Test Training

Until the last week before the hunt test, you shouldn't vary your training program or schedule at all. Train just as frequently as ever, no more, no less. Keep your training sessions the same length as always, and above all, don't "train him into the ground" with extremely long sessions full of extra pressure. Continue working on the same problems in the same way. Of course, it would probably help if you could train in a few new places, especially when you do your hunt test simulations. But, in general, just keep doing what you've been doing all along. If what you've been doing has worked well enough to get your dog ready for this upcoming hunt test, it will keep him ready, too.

However, during the last week before the hunt test, you should lighten up substantially. Simplify your tests to ensure consistent success and heap on the praise and petting each time he succeeds. Shorten your training sessions so that he still wants more when you head for home. If you feel he needs more exercise, let him take romps after each training session. Walk along and watch him so he doesn't get into trouble, but otherwise just let him run free and do whatever he wants. Then play with him a few minutes before loading him up in your vehicle and heading for home. You want him confident and happy when you heel him to the line at the hunt test, so you should build that confidence and happiness as much as possible during this final week.

🐾 Finding a Hunt Test

If you belong to a club and a training group, you'll almost certainly learn where and when hunt tests of your chosen venue are held every year. In each format, the sponsoring organization (AKC, UKC/HRC, NAHRA, or CKC) assigns each club one or two "dates" per year (typically several months apart) and refuses to grant those same dates to other clubs within a certain radius. This protects each club from reduced entries due to nearby competing tests. A "date" is a weekend in the year, numbered from the first weekend of January to the last weekend of December. Each club gets the same numbered weekends each year, but not the same calendar dates. For example, the first weekend in January may be January 1 and 2, January 6 and 7,

ꔭ Reread the Rule Book

or any two calendar days between. This fluctuation in early January affects the sequential number of all following weekends, as does the presence or absence of February 29 (Leap Day). Thus, each club's "dates" are the same sequential weekend year in and year out, although the actual calendar dates vary.

Most clubs conduct their tests on Saturday and Sunday, but some begin on Friday or extend to Monday, for one reason or another.

If you are unfamiliar with test schedules in your area, go to the sponsoring organization's website (see the Appendix), where you'll find a complete, nationwide schedule of tests, giving the dates, general location, and contact information for the test secretary. Contact the test secretary for entry forms (or on-line entry instructions). Check the closing date, after which entries will not be accepted. To avoid sending your entry too late, submit it as soon as you're sure you'll be making the trip.

One very important point, which I've occasionally forgotten (much to my regret): Get a detailed map that shows you how to get to the test site. Most clubs try to put up adequate direction signs on the roads around the test site, but "adequate" for a native and "adequate" for a non-native, particularly one (like me) with zero navigational instincts are two entirely different things. Once, when unable to find a site, I decided to follow a pickup camper that looked like it might belong to a dog person. I followed this truck off the highway, then off the blacktop, then off the gravel road, and finally onto what was little more than a cow trail. I bounced along behind this pickup for a mile or so before it stopped. A man got out, started rigging up a fishing rod, and looked at me as though he thought I was trying to steal his "honey hole." So I rambled back whence I had come and eventually found the grounds. Another time, I spent about an hour looking for the site when I knew I had to be quite close to it. I turned this way and that, going in several big circles on dirt roads. Finally, I found a road I hadn't tried before and said to myself, "Okay, if it's not down here, to heck with it! I'm going home!" I turned, drove over a hill, and before I'd gone fifty more yards, people were yelling at me because I had driven right into the middle of a test while a dog was running. Hoo-boy! As I said, get a detailed map and very specific directions on how to get to the test site. As a precaution, the day before the test (perhaps after you check into your motel), you should make a dry run to the test grounds, not only to make sure you can find it, but also to see how long it takes to get there.

Your entry forms will come with literature about nearby motels, restaurants, and so forth. If you plan to stay in a motel, reserve your room early. When you do, ask if they accept dogs. Granted, the literature you receive should list only motels in which pets are welcome. However, motels change policies from time to time, so it's always best to check on this personally. You should also check on the availability of nearby areas where you can exercise and air your dog. Some motels have spacious grounds, while others are jammed into a complex of businesses. In this latter case you would have to drive some distance for canine exercising and airing.

Filling in an entry form is quite simple, but exceedingly aggravating because it requires all sorts of information from your dog's registration certificate, information you probably have to look up each time. If the host club offers on-line entries, as more and more of them do, you need enter this information only once for all clubs that use the same on-line entry service, since the service saves your entry data for use in future entries of the same dog in later tests.

For clubs that don't use one of these services, I've developed my own little shortcut to filling out the entry form. On my computer, I created my own entry form, with all the appropriate information about my dog and myself, but with blanks for the name of the host club, the date and location of the test. When I receive an entry form in the mail (or from the host club's website), I fill in the club name, and so on, on my computer's entry form, print it, and send it off. That's much easier than filling in all the data about my dog and myself. I have an entry form for each dog. When I get a new dog, I simply make a copy of another dog's entry form and change the appropriate information. If you use this process, be sure to make your form the proper size for the hunt tests you enter, and key in any "legally required" words the sponsoring organization may need (which you can find on any regular entry form). Incidentally, host club test secretaries love my computer-produced entry forms because they can read everything on them so easily, unlike so many of the handwritten ones they receive.

If you mail your entry form, don't forget to enclose a check for the amount of the entry fee. If you forget this, you may get an unpleasant surprise when you arrive at the test grounds, namely, that your dog isn't entered and you've wasted a trip. Host clubs try to contact people who forget to enclose checks, but they're only human and do make mistakes.

As soon as entries close, the host club has a "drawing" for each testing level, in which they draw the entered dogs' names from a hat to determine the sequence in which the dogs will run in the first series. If the host club has a website, they'll post the results of this draw, so you can learn your dog's number ahead of time. That tells you how many dogs are scheduled to run before your turn. For example, if your dog is number 8, seven dogs are scheduled to run ahead of him. Of course, they may not all show up—either on time or at all—so don't plan too much on running in exactly that sequence.

"Scratch" policies have become quite complicated in recent years. In the early days, if you notified the host club before the drawing that your entered dog would not be there, they considered it a "withdrawal" and refunded your entire entry fee. However, if you so notified the host club after the drawing, they considered it a "scratch" (because they had to scratch your dog's name off the list of starters) and they refunded your entry fee less a small "scratch fee" (usually about $10). Clubs justified this fee due to the fact that, after the draw, the club had firmed up the test and spent money on birds, etc., and so would lose money if they refunded the entire entry fee for scratches. Today, clubs call any withdrawn dog a "scratch," whether he was withdrawn before or after the drawing. Moreover, each club has its own policy regarding how much and under what circumstances they will refund. Most clubs explain their "scratch" policy in the literature that comes with their entry forms. Read it and hope you don't have to use it. However, if after entering you find you won't be able to make it to the test, contact the test secretary and hope you can persuade him to refund at least part of your entry fee. *Nota bene:* If, without informing the host club ahead of time, you simply fail to show up for the test, you're considered a "no-show," and you probably won't get a dime back, no matter how well you plead your case.

🐾Preparing for the Trip

To run in a hunt test, you will often have to drive many miles and stay two or three nights in a motel. Before leaving home, you should make a checklist of all the items you will need for yourself and your dog, both on the trip and at the test. If you leave something behind, you may not be able to replace it en route or at your destination.

For yourself, you need plenty of clothing, because the weather may change while you're away. You need hunt test clothes and footwear in various weights. Some should be water repellant. In addition to hunt test attire, you need something appropriate for the restaurants in which you'll be eating. If you go into a restaurant all decked out in camo and it isn't hunting season, you may be mistaken for a terrorist. Once when clad in camo, I ate a nervous breakfast under the watchful eyes of two state troopers who were eating in the same restaurant. Then, too, if the host club has planned a cocktail party for all participants, you may also need some dress clothes.

If you dislike the discordant noise car radios emit these days, you may want to take some tapes or CDs along to play as you travel. If you're a reader, take along books and magazines to read at the motel and at the hunt test, during the long waits between runs. You might also want to take some refreshments (coffee, munchies, and so forth) to eat while traveling. You should take along a large ice chest, filled with ice and whatever provisions you need to make your own lunch at the test grounds, in case you can't leave long enough to go to a nearby restaurant. Take sunblock, paper towels, toilet paper, and hand soap.

Don't forget your dog-related equipment, such as collars, leads, crates, tie-out stakes and chains, food and water bowls. If you use an e-collar in training, take it along, even though you can't use it while on the test grounds. When you exercise your dog away from the test grounds, you may want to put the e-collar on him as a safety precaution. For airing him on the test grounds, you should have a long leash of some kind. For this, I prefer a long retractable lead.

Above all, don't forget your lanyard and whistles (plus back-ups, just in case). If you leave them at home, you may have trouble borrowing someone else's. No one wants to share whistles.

For your dog, take along plenty of food and water. If you forget his food, you may not be able to buy the same brand near the test, and any other brand could make him sick. Many dogs suffer very loose bowels for a few days after a change in food. Dogs are also quite sensitive to changes in water. I usually bring two large (three- to five-gallon) containers of water from home. I leave one in my motel room and take the other with me to the test. That way, I'm always prepared.

While away from home, feed your dog lightly two or three times a day and give him plenty of exercise immediately after each meal. Dogs have died in their crates at tests and trials because they ate large meals, drank copious amounts of water, and then rolled around inside their crates. Their intestines, filled with water-swollen food, twisted around and bloated, killing them.

🐾 At the Motel

As soon as you check in, find out whether the motel restaurant will be open in time for your breakfast, and if not, where you might be able to find one that is. I've had an occasional unpleasant surprise on the first morning of a test, discovering that the motel restaurant opened quite late on weekends.

While at the motel, you should keep your dog crated, either in your room or in your vehicle (properly ventilated), except when exercising him. Since I run only one or two dogs, I prefer crating them in my room, where I can keep an eye on them. People who let their dogs run loose in a motel room are largely responsible for the growing number of motels that refuse to accept guests with pets. Also, by keeping my dogs in my room, I can keep them quiet. Out in my truck, they could be barking and thus disturbing other guests without my knowing it. When I go out to eat, I usually take my dogs with me and leave them (locked) in the well-ventilated dog box on my truck while I'm in the restaurant. If I were to leave them in my room, they might bark at the unusual sounds outside the room and disturb other guests.

As soon as I've moved into my motel room, I exercise my dogs in the nearest available area. I also exercise them after they eat and before I go to bed for the night.

Chapter 6
General Handling Guidelines

GENERAL DOG CARE

Exercising and Airing

Each morning before heading to the test grounds, you should give your dog a good run. Go to a field near your motel, strap your e-collar on him (just in case), and turn him loose for perhaps fifteen minutes. Of course, watch him closely lest he get lost or into trouble somehow.

Failing to do this each morning can precipitate performance problems in the first series, such as taking a "romp" or breaking. An inadequately exercised dog may take a romp on the go-bird of the first series. After reaching the area of the fall and locating the bird, he feigns ignorance while running in merry circles around and around, more or less within the area of the fall, until he feels physically relieved. Only then does he rush in, pick up the bird, and bring it to the boss. This retrieve may technically be a success, but the romp forces judges to penalize the dog. This has happened to me several times. In 1975, my inadequately exercised Golden, Duffy (Duncan Dell's MacDuff** CD) took a romp on the go-bird of the first series of the day and failed to place, although he did receive a J.A.M. (Judges Award of Merit). In 1977, I again ran a dog without properly exercising him first. Brandy (Rumrunner's Brandy***) took a romp on the go-bird of the first series of the day, for which the judges told me later they dropped him from first to third place. In field trial jargon, that romp cost us the trial! More recently, in a level 3 hunt test, my inadequately exercised Golden, Gamble (KC's Take'n A Chance** MH), broke on the second bird of a triple in the first series and thereby eliminated himself. Failing to exercise a dog properly each morning before the first series is an easy mistake to make, especially when you're traveling to distant hunt tests. Perhaps my repeated mental lapses in this regard will help you avoid that particular mistake and will encourage you to give your dog a good run before the first series every day. Ideally, you should do this away from the test grounds, so the presence of other dogs won't hinder you. Frequently, you will be able to find a large, open field near your motel.

I've also calmed a dog before the first series by having him hold a dead bird for several minutes. Many years ago, before hunt tests began, I did this with my field trial Golden, Brandy. We had a mini motor home, so I'd take him inside and have him sit holding a dead duck three or four times for perhaps five minutes each. That settled this very hyper animal down to something approaching canine rationality. More recently, I did something similar with my hunt test German Shorthair, Erick (Westwind's Erick Von Greif, MH). Shortly before his brace was called, I heeled him about for a few minutes while he carried a dead quail, which calmed him down as much as anything could. If you have an unusually high-strung dog, you might try some version of this technique before the first series. Of course, follow the rules and do it away from the hunt test grounds.

While at the test, your dog will be confined much more than he is at home. Whenever you're not running him, you'll have to confine him either in his crate or on a stakeout chain. If you don't occasionally take him off somewhere away from the grounds and let him exercise for a reasonable length of time, he'll suffer a canine form of "cabin fever," which, when aggravated by the excitement of the hunt test environment, may well wind his spring more tightly than you want.

You should, of course, "air" your dog shortly before he runs in each series. Most clubs set up areas for this, but because of the presence of other dogs, you may have to air on lead. For such situations, to give my dog maximum freedom, I use a long retractable lead. Some dogs balk at airing on lead and then relieve their bladders and bowels while working and under judgment, which is a real aggravation to all concerned, besides being anything but a big plus on the dog's scorecard. To avoid this, in training sessions "practice" airing on lead frequently, to accustom him to relieving himself that way. You might consider this a form of canine "potty training." (And you thought retriever training was all about birds!)

🐾Food and Water

If you normally feed your dog twice a day, morning and evening, you should do the same while at a hunt test. Of course, you shouldn't feed him within an hour or so before he has to run a series. You should water him as often as he needs it. However, as mentioned before, you should never confine him in his crate immediately after feeding and watering him. If he rolls around inside, the water-soaked and therefore expanded food in his stomach can twist his intestines and bring on "bloat," which can kill him very quickly. I know more than one person who has suffered through that experience. *Verba sapientibus!* (Words for the wise!)

FOR EACH SERIES 🐾

🐾The Judges' Instructions

You should arrive at the location of each series in plenty of time to hear the judges' instructions and watch the test dog run. Before running a test dog in each series, one of the judges will explain the hunting scenario and perhaps will say a few words about what they expect of the dogs and handlers in the test. If you have any questions, be polite and save them until the judge finishes giving his instructions, even if other handlers are rude and interrupt the judge. Ask your questions clearly and concisely. Don't embellish them with your own hunting yarns or personal observations on the test.

A caution: Don't let anything the judge says induce you to make an unnecessary change in your handling technique. I once blew an AKC master level spaniel hunt test because I tried to take advantage of the judge's generosity. This judge said she'd allow two post-flush whistles to stop the dog. Like most spaniel folks, I had always done nicely with only one whistle immediately after the flush, but this unexpected judicial gift was irresistible. So far so good. But I went further and decided to save those two whistles until I absolutely needed them. Bad decision! In our first series run, my English Springer, Flick (Orion's Flicker, MH), flushed a rooster pheasant and then sat down as nicely as you please. However, since I "saved" the whistle I usually tooted at that time, Flick figured I was giving him permission to break and chase, which he did. I then used that whistle, and he stopped, but it was too late. He had already eliminated himself by breaking after hupping (sitting) automatically at the flush. Please note: I wasn't following any judicial instruction. I was experimenting with a wild idea the judge's instructions had suggested to my hunt-test-hyped mind. Don't make that mistake. Handle your dog in a hunt test exactly as you do in training. If you do anything else, you'll confuse him and he may well bomb out, like Flick did.

Of course, if the judges' instructions were to indicate that they won't allow something you normally do or if they insist on something you normally don't do, you'd have a different situation. In such a situation, if what they require is within the rules, you have no choice but to follow their instructions. If what they require is not within the rules, you should point this out to them, perhaps doing so tactfully with a question. Frankly, I've never seen anything like this happen, so you shouldn't fret about it.

The Test Dog

After giving their instructions, the judges will call a test dog to the line to demonstrate the test. Generally speaking, judges select test dogs that are at approximately the same level of training as the dogs entered in the testing level. That way, the handlers can see what sort of problems dogs at that level are apt to have with the test. Therefore, you should watch the test dog carefully before each series. Granted, in level 1, you're pretty limited in what you can do to help your dog deal with whatever hazards each test presents, but you should at least be aware of them. You should pay particular attention to the procedure at the line—that is, how the test dog handler gets to the line, what interaction (if any) he has with the judges, whether the judges let the handler indicate when he's ready or they simply call for the birds as soon as he and his dog arrive at the line, ready or not.

Let the Games Begin!

Immediately after the test dog runs, the marshal will call the first dog to the line. If yours is the first dog, you have a problem. You need to watch the test dog run, but for obvious reasons you're not allowed to have your dog there watching with you. If the holding blind is sufficiently close to the line, you might be able to see the test dog run from there, with your dog beside you but unable to watch the test. If that isn't possible for whatever reason (perhaps the holding blind is too far from the line, is behind a bush, or something like that), you should tell the marshal early on that you're running first, but you'll need time after the test dog runs to go to your vehicle, get your dog, and return. Then do exactly that, and don't rush yourself or your dog. Both of you need to approach the line calmly and deliberately, not in a frenzied panic. After watching the test dog, you have the right to a reasonable amount of time in which to bring your dog to the line. After all, as the first handler, you need to see the test dog run more than any of the other handlers, each of whom will be able to watch one or more preceding dogs run before going to the line. Occasionally, the first handler will have a friend or family member keep his dog on lead close to the line, but where the dog can't see the test. That way, after the test dog runs, the handler must go only a short distance to pick up his dog and head for the line. This may work for the calmer, more experienced dog, but I wouldn't recommend it for anyone with an inexperienced dog, especially a high-roller that suffers easily from separation anxiety. Such unnecessary stimulation immediately before running could cause the dog to perform poorly and fail the test.

If you're not one of the first few dogs, you should hang around the line and watch as many dogs run as you can. This will tattoo the procedure to be followed onto your subconscious, and give you a better idea of where the hazards are and how difficult the test is.

As your turn approaches, give yourself plenty of time to get back to your vehicle, air your dog one last time, and go to the holding blind. Air your dog on lead, for there may be other dogs in the same general area, and not all dogs are friendly. Heel your dog to the holding blind on lead. By so doing, you are reminding him that he's now entering a controlled situation and that you are in charge. Once in the holding blind, make him sit quietly beside you until the marshal summons you to the line.

At no time, especially before you run, and even more especially while you're waiting in a holding blind, should you criticize the test.

Many years ago, I watched a young pro embarrass himself this way at a field trial. Because he was running dog number one that day, he waited in the holding blind while three test dogs failed the test. However, he didn't see any of them run because he was facing the gallery explaining to one and all that the test was too easy, would prove nothing, and was just a waste of time. You guessed it: His dog failed the test even more miserably than any of the three test dogs! When he returned from the line and walked past the gallery, he had his hat pulled down over his eyes, and he walked with a slump he hadn't had earlier.

You should never offer unsolicited advice to other handlers. If someone asks you a question, answer it, of course, but if no one asks you can safely assume that no one wants your opinion. Let me repeat: *Unsolicited advice is usually worth far less than you pay for it.*

While your dog is working, concentrate on him so you'll be able to respond quickly if he needs your help. If the judges ask you any questions, answer them, of course, but don't initiate a conversation with them and above all don't explain your dog's work to them. Many years ago, I slipped into this habit during our monthly (and highly informal) fun trials. As my dog worked, I gave the judges a running commentary on what he was doing and why. I did that until I once ran under Jane Laman. After I said a few words, she said quite firmly, "Jim, you just handle your dog and let us decide what he's doing!" She was right, so I shut up. Later, I decided that the next time I ran under her, I'd come to the line with a very large cork in my mouth. However, before I could do that, she turned pro and therefore had to stop judging. Oh, well.

If the judges tell you to pick up your dog, they've decided to drop him for whatever mistake he has made. Don't argue. Don't protest. Simply pick him up, thank the judges, and heel your miscreant back to your vehicle. If you're confused about why they dropped him, ask them later, after the last dog runs the series. Why thank the judges when they've dropped your dog? Because that's a courtesy you should always extend as you leave the line, even when you dislike the test and your dog's performance has embarrassed you. Judging is (pardon the awful pun) a thankless job, as you'll probably find out someday.

Pro Lonny Taylor heels his Lab to the line while judge Pat Corcoran looks on.

Leaving the Line

In every series, you're under judgment until you've heeled your dog away from the line and back some distance behind the judges. Until then, if you're careless, you can still blow it all. As a precaution, when you turn to heel your dog off line, you should turn toward him. That way, you block him with your legs, so he's less likely to bolt unexpectedly away from you and get into mischief. If you turn away from him, several bad things could happen. For example, if you have just honored, the working dog may be returning to the line with (or without) a bird, in which case your dog might decide to confront or socialize with him, thereby interfering with the working dog. If you turn away from him after working, he might decide to check out the birds on the drying rack or get acquainted with the next dog coming to the line. And so on. Granted, every rule has exceptions, but this one should apply in most instances.

As soon as you're no longer under judgment, put a slip lead on your dog to prevent him from doing anything foolish. If a live bird

Pro Lonny Taylor heels his Lab away from the line after running a test under judges Pat Corcoran and Rich Sinclair. Two other handlers wait their turns to run in the two holding blinds. Notice that judge Pat Corcoran is still holding the duck and gun that Lonny handed him as he left the line.

were to escape and run past you toward the judges, who could blame your bird-crazy dog for trying to "help out"? Once, when I had heeled my Golden, Gamble, on lead a long ways from the line after we ran a test, a duck escaped from one of the bird crates and started running and flapping, but not flying. I volunteered to have Gamble catch it for the bird steward. That was almost a big mistake, for that bird led Gamble on quite a chase. He finally caught the duck and brought it to me, but only after I had had horrible visions of the duck leading Gamble back into the middle of the test while another dog was working. We would have been eliminated, and it would have been my fault, not Gamble's.

Before you confine your dog in his crate again, you should walk him around on lead for a few minutes. While walking him around, tell him what a fine fellow he is, even if he could have been a whole lot "finer" in the series he just completed. Give him a drink and let him air. If possible, put him on a tie-out chain for a few minutes. You do all this so he won't figure that, as soon as he delivers the last bird, he'll be immediately confined again. That can negatively affect his attitude while running.

The Callbacks

After you run the first series (and every series thereafter), unless you're absolutely sure that your dog has failed the test and will be dropped or there are many dogs yet to run, you shouldn't go too far from the test site. You should be present for the callbacks, when the marshal announces the numbers of the dogs that the judges have called back to run the next series. If you and your dog are called back, follow the marshal to the location of the next series. Again, arrive there in time to hear the judges' instructions and to watch the test dog run the test.

If your dog's number is not called, and you aren't sure why he was dropped, ask the marshal to double-check his list to make sure your number isn't on it. Even marshals make mistakes! If he confirms that you indeed weren't called back and you're still puzzled, ask the marshal when would be a good time for you to approach the judges and learn what you or your dog did wrong. When you talk to the judges, avoid any hint of confrontation. Simply ask them why they dropped your dog, listen to their responses, say "Thank you," and leave. Don't try rebutting their explanation, and don't ask argumentative questions. If you really don't understand their reasons, ask them if they would explain them to you more fully after the last series. Most judges will do this, taking as long as necessary, provide you're seeking information and not questioning their judgment or, worse, their honesty!

I once ran in a pointing dog hunt test in which my bracemate's previous dog had failed. I had seen the dog run and felt the judges were absolutely correct in dropping him. But in our brace, all the way around the back course, this guy argued with the judges about their decision on his other dog. The judges were very polite, answering his every objection most patiently. He kept changing tactics, offering new and ever more ridiculous excuses. Through it all, the judges remained calm, which was fortunate for that handler. A few years earlier, one of those judges had been a four-time state champion in high school wrestling and was then a high school wrestling coach. As I listened to that handler's ravings, I found myself hoping that judge would jump off his horse and "persuade" the mouthy griper to say uncle at least once, and perhaps several times. But he didn't. I was some distance from disappointed when this guy's second dog also loused up in the bird field and failed to qualify.

I haven't agreed with the decisions of every judge I've run under, but I've never argued with any of them. If I'm really steamed, I say nothing to anyone, but simply hop in my truck and leave the test grounds, at least for a while. While away, I recall all the times I've felt the judges had erred the other way, by being kinder to my dog than I would have been if I had been judging. I also recall some of the close decisions I've had to make as a judge, a few of which I've worried about the next day. I remember the times I've had to drop some of my friends' dogs, worrying momentarily that it might affect our friendship. It never has. All in all, judging is too tough for any judge to have to endure abuse from a handler. When you sent in your entry, you knew who the judges would be, and you in effect paid for their evaluation of your dog. If, after you run under them, you seriously disagree with their decision, simply don't run under them anymore.

THE AWARDS

After the last series, proceed to wherever the marshal says the rosettes will be passed out. If you receive one, thank the judges, and then remain modestly quiet, even if you're almost exploding with pride and want to tell everyone what a great dog you have and what a great trainer you are.

If you don't receive a rosette and don't understand why, after all the rosettes have been passed out approach the judges and ask them what you or your dog did wrong. Again, don't challenge their judgment. Listen to their explanation and whether or not you agree, thank them and walk away. Arguing, especially after the hunt test is over, will gain you a bad reputation, but nothing else.

After the rosettes have been passed out, if you liked the tests, by all means tell the judges. Do this whether or not your dog qualified. They'll appreciate your kind words so much, especially if your dog failed but you still found their tests worthy of a compliment. After returning home, I've frequently dropped a short note to judges whose tests I liked (whether or not my dog qualified). I once did this after my dog bombed out in the first series, and I later heard that judges really appreciate notes under such circumstances. Perhaps if more handlers did such things more often, it would persuade good judges to keep on judging in spite of all the whining they often have to listen to.

Chapter 7
Marking Tests

BACKGROUND INFORMATION

Marked retrieves, or more simply "marks," can be singles, doubles, or triples. In a single mark (or "single"), only one bird is thrown before the handler may send his dog. In a double mark (or "double"), two birds are thrown, one at a time, in different locations before the handler may send his dog. The first bird thrown (and normally the last retrieved) is called the "memory bird," because the dog must remember it while retrieving the other bird. The last bird thrown (and normally the first retrieved) is called the "go-bird." In a triple mark (or "triple"), three birds are thrown, one at a time, in three different locations before the handler may send his dog. The first two birds thrown are called "memory birds," and the last bird thrown is called the "go-bird."

The term "go-bird" has an interesting history. Before hunt tests began, field trialers called the last bird down in a multiple mark the "diversion bird," or more simply, the "diversion," because it diverted the dog's attention from the memory bird(s). However, hunt testers introduced a new type of "diversion bird," namely one thrown as the dog returns with a bird from another retrieve. Thus, retriever folks needed a new name for the older type of diversion bird, the last one down in a multiple mark. Someone (I have no idea who) figured that, since the dog "goes" shortly after the last bird is down, we should call that last bird the "go-bird." The term stuck and has been used ever since, in both hunt tests and field trials.

A marking test can be on land, in water, or some combination of the two. Marking tests can be run with or without accompanying blind retrieves. In almost all tests that include both marks and blinds, the dog picks up all the marks before running the blind(s). The only exception is the "poison bird" test, which I discuss in Chapter 8.

The start of a marking test. The judge is signaling for a throw; the handler is shouldering her gun; the other judge and the next two handlers (in holding blinds) watch.

A marking test can be either a "regular" or a "walk-up." In a regular marking test, the handler and dog assume fixed positions before the first bird goes up. Normally, the dog sits beside the handler, who stands or sits at the line, but sometimes the dog may have to sit some distance away from his handler. Normally (but not always), the handler indicates to the judges when he and his dog are ready before a judge calls for the birds to be thrown. In a walk-up marking test, the handler heels his dog from a starting position toward the line and, as they near the line, a judge signals for the birds to be thrown. When the birdcall or shot for the first bird sounds, the handler may command his dog, by voice or whistle, to sit.

Honoring

All honoring is done in marking tests. In such a test, two handlers and their dogs are at the line and under judgment. The dog that actually retrieves the birds is the "working dog." While the working dog makes his retrieves, the "honoring dog" remains in place until one of

Honoring in a regular marking test. The handler on the left has the working dog; the handler on the right has the honoring dog.

Honoring in a walk-up marking test. The handler on the left is heeling the working dog; the handler on the right is heeling the honoring dog. The judges are walking along behind them.

the judges releases him, which usually happens after the working dog is well on his way to the go-bird. Normally (but not always), each dog works first and then honors while the next dog works. Honoring can be incorporated into either a regular or a walk-up marking test. In the former, the honoring dog and his handler assume a position several yards to one side or the other of the working dog and remain there until released. In a walk-up test, the honoring dog's handler heels his dog on a path parallel to and several yards to one side or the other of the path of the working dog and his handler. When the birdcall or shot for the first bird sounds, both handlers may command their dogs to sit by voice or whistle command.

🐾 Diversions

In hunt tests, you can encounter two types of diversions: diversion shots and diversion birds.

When one of the "guns" out in the field fires a shot without a bird being thrown, he is firing a diversion shot. Judges use diversion shots to distract the working dog. Most diversion shots occur in blind retrieve tests (see Chapter 8), but they are sometimes used in marking tests.

Diversion birds can also be used in either blind retrieve or marking tests. When used in blinds, they're usually "poison birds." When used in a double marking tests, the bird is thrown as the dog returns with the go-bird. When used in a triple marking tests, although the bird usually is thrown as the dog returns with the go-bird, it may also be thrown as he returns with the first of the two memory birds. Diversion birds tempt the dog to switch, that is, to drop the bird he's carrying and go after the diversion bird. They also put pressure on the dog's memory, for the dog normally retrieves the diversion bird next, immediately after delivering the bird he was carrying when the diversion bird went up. That "extra retrieve" delays the retrieve of one or both memory birds, thereby taxing the dog's memory.

Nota bene: A diversion bird is not judged as a mark, which means you can handle your dog (with whistle and arm signals) to it without penalty! Why? Your dog sees the diversion bird while he's still out in the field, but you send him to retrieve it from the line. Things look considerably different from the line, so judges cannot expect dogs to mark diversion birds like marks they see from the line.

🐾 Guns

The helpers out in the field who blow the birdcalls, shoot popper shells, throw birds, and shoot fliers are collectively called "guns."

Thus, we say that the judge signals to the guns when he wants the mark to be thrown. It normally takes two such guns for a control bird mark: One blows the birdcall and shoots while the other one throws the birds or operates the bird-launching device. It takes at least three guns for a flier: One blows the birdcall and throws the bird while the other two shoot the bird as it flies away.

🐾 Fliers

A flier is a live bird that is thrown and then shot by the guns in a marking test. Fliers add realism to the test. They also tempt the dog to break more than does a control bird (see below). Because fliers are live and can behave somewhat erratically, the fliers thrown and shot at one station may fall in a variety of places over a rather wide area. This puts a lot of bird scent in the area of the fall, which can help or hurt dogs that run late, depending on where their birds fall. If a flier falls a long way from where the majority of fliers have fallen, all that old scent may keep a dog from driving deep enough or wide enough to find his bird. To equalize the test for all dogs, most judges have several fliers shot to fall in the area before the first dog runs.

🐾 Control Birds

A control bird is a dead bird thrown in a marking test. Since these birds are dead, the guns can control where they fall, throw after throw, thereby giving each dog approximately the same fall. They lack the excitement of fliers, but they do allow more uniform testing of all dogs. They also allow the host club to cut expenses by re-using birds multiple times. In most hunt tests, only one or two series per testing level will include a flier; all the rest of the marks will be control birds.

🐾 Handling on a Mark

"Handling" has two meanings: Sometimes it is a general term meaning everything the human half of the team does; other times it's a specific term meaning the whistle and arm signals the handler uses to direct his dog to a blind retrieve or to a mark the dog has forgotten or mismarked. Here we use the term in this second sense, that is, "handling on a mark," via whistle and arm signals.

To succeed in hunt test marking tests, you must know when to let your dog hunt for a bird on his own and when to toot the Sit-whistle and handle him to the bird. For this, you need to understand a critical concept, namely, *the area of the fall.*

Since no dog "pins" or "steps on" every mark, we must allow all dogs a certain amount of geography around each marked bird (or "fall") in which he may legitimately hunt. We call that allowable space the "area of the fall." As long as a dog hunts within that area, he's doing a good job and should not be handled. If he strays out of that area for more than a few seconds, he is said to be "disturbing too much cover," in which case his handler should intervene and handle him to the bird. Such "handling on a mark" is always a fault, but letting the dog disturb too much cover is a worse fault.

Unfortunately, we can only approximate the area of the fall for any particular mark. We cannot give a precise definition with which all retriever folks will agree. As you gain experience, your judgment of this nebulous but crucial concept will improve. Until it does, you should rely on the advice of your trusty mentor. When he's not around to guide you, the following general rules will help.

For a single mark and for the go-bird of a multiple mark, on a relatively windless day, the area of the fall is a circle around the bird with a diameter roughly 20 percent of the distance from the line to the bird. Thus, for a 100-yard single mark or go-bird, the circle would have a diameter of twenty yards. For a fifty-yard mark, the diameter would be ten yards, and so forth. Now, since dogs search with their noses more than with their eyes, any significant wind will affect both the location and the shape of the area of the fall. A strong wind would change it into a teardrop-shaped area with the bird at the small end of the teardrop. Such an area allows the dog to hunt the downwind side of the bird, which is where the wind pushes the "scent cone." In a light wind, the area of the fall would be a slightly deformed circle, shifted somewhat to the downwind side of the bird, and so on.

For the second retrieve in a multiple mark, the area of the fall would be about 25 percent larger than it would be for the same mark as a single or go-bird. Thus, for a relatively windless 100-yard mark, it would be a circle with a twenty-five yard diameter, and so forth.

For the third retrieve in a multiple mark, the area of the fall would be about 50 percent larger than it would be for the same mark as a single or go-bird. Thus for a windless 100-yard mark, it would be a circle with a thirty-yard diameter, and so forth.

Please understand, these are just first-cut approximations, not mathematically precise definitions. As such, they will help you get started in estimating an appropriate area of the fall for any mark. But you shouldn't use them to argue with your mentor or, worse still, with judges.

Now, as long as your dog is hunting purposefully within the area of a fall, let him hunt undisturbed. He'll get more credit for a long "area hunt" than he would for being handled to the bird. However, if he wanders from the area for more than a few seconds, toot the Sit-whistle and start waving your arms about to direct him to the bird. And handle him all the way to the bird, not just back into the area of the fall for more hunting. Once you blow the Sit-whistle, you've told the judges that your dog needs help (which they already knew, of course), so he'll get no credit for resuming his hunt after you handle him back into the area. In fact, he'll probably be knocked down a bit for the unnecessary delay. Therefore, after you blow the Sit-whistle, you should handle him exactly as you would in a blind retrieve. For suggestions on how to do this, refer to Chapter 8.

SINGLE MARKS

In hunt tests, you'll encounter single marks mostly in level 1 tests, in which doubles and triples are not allowed by the rules of any format. Level 3 judges sometimes use single marks as "poison birds" in blind retrieve tests (covered in Chapter 8), but most singles are in level 1. Therefore, the entire presentation here assumes that the test is in level 1.

Setting up at the Line

First off, don't try to be a hero. Use whatever advantages the rules allow and whatever leeway the judges permit. For example, at this

In level 1 tests, when you are allowed to restrain your dog, do so! Here Jim Spencer demonstrates the proper use of a belt cord for that purpose.

level most formats allow you to heel your dog to and from the line on lead and to restrain him there until the judge calls your number. Even if your dog is an international obedience trial champion, heel him to the line on lead! Ditto for restraining him at the line. Even if he's as steady as a patio statue, restrain him in whatever way is legal. Forget about showing him off for everyone present, especially the judges. Look at it this way: If you don't use the lead while heeling and don't restrain him at the line, he'll get no extra credit, even if he's a perfect gentleman. Nor will you impress anyone there, least of all the judges, since everyone present has seen more good heeling and steady dogs than they can remember. On the other hand, if your wonder-dog goes out of control on the way to the line because he's off lead, he'll be penalized, perhaps severely. Worse still, if he breaks because you didn't restrain him, the judges have no choice but to drop him, no matter how well he marks the bird, no matter how stylishly he performs, no matter how nicely he delivers. If he breaks, he's out, period. Thus, such showboating can gain you nothing and cost you everything. When the best you can do is break even, why gamble?

At the line, set your dog up facing the mark. Granted, even if the "guns" are visible, you cannot point them out to him as many field trialers do, but you can at least set him up facing in their general direction. That way, he'll more easily see the fall and he'll be lined up to run toward it when you send him. Once he's properly set up (and settled down), signal to the judges that you're ready. If your dog is sitting on your left side, you should do this by flicking your right hand behind

Two live guns shoot a just thrown live bird for a marking test.

your back. One of the judges will then signal to the guns, who will make an initial sound (birdcall or shot) and then throw the bird. If it's a control bird, they'll fire a popper shell. If it's a flier, they'll actually shoot it.

Sending Your Dog

As soon as the bird hits the ground (or water), stop looking at the bird and turn your attention totally to your dog, so you can read him properly. Remember to wait for the judge to call your number before sending him. If you send him before that, he'll be charged with breaking and will be dropped. On the other hand, you needn't send him as soon as the judge calls your number. *Look at your dog's head.* If he isn't properly locked in on the fall, give him time to refocus on it before sending him. If you send him when he's looking the wrong way, he'll go the wrong way, and may never get near the bird. By knowing when to send him and when to wait you'll help him succeed, which is your only purpose at the line.

Let Him Hunt!

If your dog has to hunt the area awhile, you may, in your anxiety to get the bird, be tempted to take charge of the situation and handle him to the bird. Don't do it unless you absolutely have to; that is, unless he hunts outside the area of the fall for more than a few seconds or starts to return to you without the bird. As long as he's hunting aggressively within the area of the fall, just stand there, bite your lip, and keep your whistle out of your mouth. Act nonchalant, even if you're just this side of complete mental collapse. That way, you won't convey to the judges that you're uncertain about your dog's marking ability, as you surely will if you pace around, mutter, and fuss.

Delivering the Bird

Whoopee! Your brilliant beastie has found the bird (with or without your help) and is bringing it to you. What should you do now? Some formats require delivery to hand, while others require only delivery to the immediate area of the handler. In this latter case, during the judges' instructions, before the test dog runs, the judges should indicate how

A Lab delivers a bird to the handler at the line.

close is close enough. If they don't, by all means, ask! (And you can't ask if you aren't there in time for the judges' instructions!)

If delivery to hand is required, as soon as your dog sits at heel, grasp the nearer end of the bird, and command "Give" (or whatever command word you use). When his mouth pops open, take the bird from him. If he "sticks" on the bird (refuses to release it), don't start a tug-of-war. That's the worst thing you could do. Instead, distract him somehow and try again. For example, you might command "Heel!" and step forward, or you might put your hand down by his head as if you were about to send him for another retrieve. Either ploy will usually trick him into releasing the bird.

If he drops the bird at your side instead of delivering it, command "Fetch!" and hope he picks it back up. If you're not sure he will do so, you might try a little technique I used years ago with my Chesapeake, Beaver (Rumrunner's Redlion Beaver, JH). Occasionally, both in training and in hunt tests, he'd sit at heel, spit the bird out, and then look up at me as if to say, "Whatcha gonna do about that, mister?" In training, I would wrestle him to the ground and force his mouth onto the bird. (Yes, he was force-broken, but he was also a Chesapeake! For Beaver, an occasional rumble seemed to satisfy some primitive Chesapeake need.) At hunt tests, where I couldn't go two falls out of three with him, I'd command "Heel!" walk him around in a tight circle, and as we approached the dropped bird, I'd say "Fetch!" and keep moving forward. As we passed the bird, he'd snatch it up and I'd take it while still moving. This wasn't pretty, but it did satisfy the requirement that he deliver to hand.

Whether or not delivery to hand is required, if your dog drops the bird some distance from you, like at the water's edge, you can only stand there, command "Fetch!" and hope he obeys. Young dogs frequently drop the bird as they emerge from water so they can more easily shake the water from their coats. If yours does this, you'll have a better chance of success if you let him shake thoroughly before commanding "Fetch!"

↳ Leaving the Line

As soon as you have the bird safely in hand, put it behind you on the side opposite your dog, and then hand it to the judge when he approaches to take it. If you were to hold it near your dog, he might start jumping and grabbing at it. If he should manage to snatch it out of your hand, you have to start the delivery process all over. You'll find it far better to get it right the first time!

Having handed the bird to one of the judges, exit the line as gracefully and quickly as possible, per the instructions on this subject in Chapter 6. As you leave, remember to thank the judges.

DOUBLE MARKS

Double marks on both land and water are required in level 2 of all formats. You may encounter an occasional double in level 3, but they're mostly a level 2 "exclusive." Therefore, the following presentation assumes that you are running your dog in level 2. Depending on the format, blind retrieves, honoring, diversion shots, and diversion birds may be incorporated with the double marks. When a blind retrieve is combined with a set of marks, the dogs pick up the marks first and then run the blind.

Level 2 doubles may be regular or walk-ups (both described above). The two differ only in what you and your dog do before the first bird goes up. Thereafter, your job on all level 2 doubles is essentially the same.

Regular Doubles

In a regular double, once you're at the line, you should set your dog up so he'll get the best possible view of both falls. Granted, you cannot point out the guns to him, as field trialers do, but you can position him advantageously. How you "maximize his visibility" at the line depends on how you normally handle him between falls. If you turn toward each bird as it's thrown and allow your dog to shift around with you, you should set him up facing the memory bird. Then, after it's down, you should turn so he will shift around to face the go-bird as it goes up. On the other hand, if you insist that your dog sit still in one place for both falls, you should position him so that he gets a very good look at the memory bird while still being able to turn his head to see the go-bird. That may be halfway between the two falls or it may be three-fourths of the way around toward the memory bird.

Don't keep your dog sitting on edge at the line any longer than necessary. As soon as he's properly positioned, signal to the judge that you're ready. (*Nota bene:* As a common courtesy, if another dog is honoring, you should first ask his handler whether he's ready.) If you're required to point a gun at each bird, as you probably will be in these tests, put the gun to your shoulder and point it properly. Don't try to cheat by holding the gun casually below shoulder level while turning your head to continue watching your dog. Incidentally, in UKC/HRC tests, you're required to fire a popper (blank) shotgun shell at each bird—and they judge gun safety stringently.

You yourself should mark the memory bird most carefully, since you're more likely to have to handle your dog on it than on the go-bird. Of course, you should also mark the go-bird, just in case.

If your dog breaks at any time, command "Heel!" with all the authority you can muster. If he returns before going too far, the judges

This handler is sending his dog for a memory bird after the dog delivered the go-bird, which the handler is holding behind his hip on the side opposite the dog.

won't drop him at this level, but will penalize him for a "controlled break." Of course, if he breaks on the memory bird, he won't get much of a look at the go-bird, so you may have to handle him to it. If he breaks on the go-bird, he should have marked both birds satisfactorily.

Remember to wait until the judge calls your number before sending your dog. Of course, you needn't send him immediately thereafter. Look at his head before sending him. If he is not properly locked in on the go-bird, pat your leg or do whatever necessary to bring his attention back to the go-bird before sending him.

🐾 Walk-Up Doubles

In a walk-up double, you first heel your dog from the holding blind to the starting position set up by the judges. Once there, have your dog sit while you remove the lead and (if required) his collar. Then, tell the judge you're ready. (As a common courtesy, if another dog is honoring, you should first ask his handler whether he's ready.) The judge will tell you to start moving forward. While heeling, don't let your dog get ahead of you, lest he break when the birds go up. Command "Heel!" as often as necessary to keep him by your side. If he forges ahead, don't move faster to keep up with him, for that will only encourage him to forge ahead faster. Instead, command "Heel!" and bring him back to you.

If you're required to point a gun at each bird, as you probably will be in these tests, put the gun to your shoulder and point it properly. Don't try to cheat by holding the gun casually while you continue watching your dog.

When the birdcall or shot that precedes the memory bird sounds, you may toot the Sit-whistle or command "Sit!" to stop your dog. If he keeps moving, repeat the command. You'll be penalized, but at least you might keep him from breaking.

After both birds are down, one of the judges will call your number, after which you can send your dog. With all the excitement, your dog may be confused about which bird to retrieve first. If so, help him focus entirely on the go-bird before you send him.

⤷When to Handle

As mentioned above, after you launch your dog for the go-bird, your job is the same for both types of double marks.

The suggestions above (under "Single Marks") on when to handle your dog for a blind retrieve on a mark also apply to doubles. As long as he is hunting aggressively within the area of the fall, let him hunt. But if he strays outside it for more than a few seconds, stop him and handle him all the way to the bird. If he appears to be about to switch, handle him as quickly as possible, for even the beginning of a switch looks bad to judges. After you've stopped him, handle him to the bird exactly as you would if it were a blind retrieve. (See the instructions in Chapter 8.)

One final point: You can easily get away with handling on one mark in a level 2 hunt test, although your dog will be penalized for failing to mark the bird. You probably won't be so fortunate if you have to handle him to a second bird during that same hunt test. Look at it this way: in a typical level 2 hunt test, your dog has to mark only four birds. If you have to handle him on one of those four, the best score he can make for marking, even if he pins the other three birds, is 75%. Now, if you have to handle him on two of those four birds, the best possible score becomes 50%, which was some distance from passing back when I was in school. Granted, not all judges are that strict, but why test their generosity unnecessarily? Clearly, as much as you can, you should "save" your handles for the later birds. In other words, on the first double mark of the day, you should hesitate a little longer before handling than you did on the last double. Of course, if your dog goes clean (no handles) on the first three marks, and if he has no "black marks" on the blinds, et cetera, you can safely handle on the last bird at the slightest provocation, if you so choose.

⤷The Deliveries

While your dog is returning with the go-bird, you should turn to face the memory bird. That way, when he sits at heel to deliver, he'll be facing his next retrieve. After he sits, you should grasp the nearer end of the bird and command "Give" (or whatever command you use). He should release his grip and back off, so that you can take possession of the bird without pulling it from his mouth.

If he drops the bird before you grasp it, command "Fetch!" At this level, he should pick it up. If he doesn't, heel him around in a tight circle and as you approach the bird, command "Fetch!" and keep moving. He'll almost certainly pick it up. That isn't pretty, but it might get you by, at least once per hunt test.

After you have the go-bird in hand, hold it behind your hip, the one opposite your dog, while you help him focus on the memory bird. As soon as he locks solidly in on it, send him. After he departs, hold the bird straight out behind you so the judge can take it. While doing this, don't take your eyes off your dog. Taking the bird is the judge's job and he can handle it even if you're not watching him.

When your dog returns with the memory bird, take it just as you did the go-bird and hold it out behind you for the judge to take. *Nota bene:* Dogs inclined to freeze and not release birds are most apt to do so on the last bird retrieved. So if yours is a "sticky" beast, be prepared to distract him in order to take the bird from him. If you put your hand down as if you're about to send him for another bird, he'll probably relax and release the bird. Or if you heel him forward and take the bird (with "Give" or whatever command you use) while still moving, he may well give it to you.

As pointed out above concerning single marks, playing tug-of-war with a sticky dog doesn't work. Many years ago, a prominent pro was handling a sticky Labrador in a field trial. The dog froze on the last bird of a triple. The pro grasped the duck's head and commanded, "Leave it!" No luck. He lifted up on the head and again commanded, "Leave it!" The dog still hung on and started rising up off his front feet. The pro lifted it higher and higher, until he held it above his head, with the dog still holding on and dangling in mid-air. Finally the duck separated, leaving the pro with the head while the dog tumbled back to earth still clinging to the carcass. As he left the line, the pro handed the head to one of the judges and said, "Sorry, but that's all I could get!"

🐾 Diversions

In level 2, you'll certainly experience diversion shots, either on the marks or the blinds. If you've used them frequently in training, your dog will probably yawn his way through them, so don't fret.

You may also encounter diversion birds. In level 2 tests, they usually will be thrown while your dog is returning with either the last mark or with a blind. Such diversion birds are intended to tempt dogs to switch. Again, if you've used them frequently in training, your dog will turn his nose up at them, as he should.

Keep in mind that a diversion bird is not a mark. Therefore, you may handle your dog to any such bird without being penalized for handling on a mark. If you mark the diversion well and if your dog handles well, you should have no problem picking up any diversion thrown for you.

✎ Honoring

Where honoring is incorporated with a double mark, each dog normally first completes the test as the working dog and then honors the work of the next dog. In level 2 tests, honoring before working may be possible, but it isn't likely.

In a regular double, after completing the marks (and blind if one is included), the handler heels his dog to the designated honoring position, which is usually several yards to one side or the other of the working dog's position. He and his dog must remain there until released by one of the judges, which normally happens after the working dog is well on his way to the go-bird.

In a walk-up double, after completing the marks (and blind if one is included), the handler heels his dog to the designated starting point for the honoring dog, which is usually several yards to one side or the other of the working dog's starting position. When the judge so indicates, both handlers heel their dogs forward until the birdcall or shot preceding the memory bird sounds, when both handlers may make their dogs sit with either a whistle or a voice command. The honoring dog and his handler must remain there until one of the judges releases them, which normally happens after the working dog is well on his way to the go-bird.

If your honoring dog breaks, command "Heel!" to bring him back. If he interferes with the working dog, he will (and should) be dropped. Similarly, if you yell loudly enough to disturb the working dog, your dog should be dropped and the working dog should be given a rerun.

If, while yours is the working dog, the honoring dog breaks but doesn't interfere with your dog, just let your dog keep on working as if nothing had happened. If the honoring dog does interfere with your dog, follow the judge's instructions (which will probably be to pick up your dog and rerun the test later). If the honoring handler's yelling distracts your dog enough so that he stops and looks back at you, you have every right to appeal to the judges for a rerun. However, if they don't grant it, you must do the best you can to get your dog to pick up this set of marks.

Leaving the Line

When you and your dog have completed the double mark test (with or without a blind retrieve and an honor), one of the judges will release you. When he does, exit gracefully and quickly, per the instructions in Chapter 6. Of course, as you leave, don't forget to thank the judges.

Triple Marks

Triple marks are a level 3 "exclusive," for they aren't allowed in the lower levels. Triples may be on land, in water, or some combination of land and water. They may include diversion shots, diversion birds, blind retrieves, and honoring. As with doubles, triples can be either regular or walk-up. The two differ only in what the handler and dog do before the first bird goes up. Thereafter, your job on all triples is essentially the same.

Regular Triples

In a regular triple, you heel your dog off lead from the holding blind to the line. Once there, you should set your dog up so he'll get the best possible view of all three falls. Although you cannot point out each set of guns to him, as field trialers do, you can position him advantageously. How you do this depends on how you normally handle him between falls. If you turn toward each bird as it's thrown and allow your dog to shift around with you, you should set him up facing the first memory bird. Then, after it's down, you should turn so he will shift around to face the other memory bird as it goes up. After it's down, you should again turn so he will shift around to face the go-bird as it goes up. On the other hand, if you insist that your dog sit still in one place for all three falls, you should position him so that he gets a very good look at both memory birds while still being able to turn his head to see the go-bird. That may be facing one or the other of the memory birds, halfway between the two memory birds, or any other position that seems advantageous, given the locations and sequence of the falls. Frankly, on widespread triples, the former handling approach (turning and having your dog shift with you) has a big advantage over the latter (making the dog sit absolutely still in one place). Of course, a shifting dog is more apt to break, so if yours has a "breaking problem," you should make him sit in one place. Most chronic breakers mark exceptionally well, in fact well enough to compensate for what they lose in mobility when forced to sit in one place through all the falls.

Don't keep your dog sitting on edge at the line any longer than necessary. When he's properly set up, signal to the judge that you're ready. (As a common courtesy, if another dog is honoring, you should first ask his handler whether he's ready.) If required to point a gun at each bird, as you probably will be in these tests, put the gun to your shoulder and point it properly. Don't try to cheat by holding the gun casually while you continue watching your dog. Incidentally, in UKC/HRC tests, you're required to fire a popper (blank) shotgun shell at each bird—and they judge gun safety stringently.

You should mark both memory birds very carefully, since you're more likely to have to handle your dog on one of them than on the go-bird. Of course, you should also mark the go-bird, just in case. Remember that, if the go-bird is one of the outside birds, your dog will probably retrieve his birds outside-outside-middle. Thus, the middle bird will be the "money bird," the one he's most apt to forget, and therefore the one you should mark exceptionally well, in case you have to handle him to it.

If your dog breaks at any time, command "Heel!" with all the authority you can muster. If he returns before going too far, he will be charged with a "controlled break." Some formats, but not all, require the judges to drop a dog for this. (You should, of course, know the rules.) If your dog breaks on either memory bird, he won't get much of a look at the remaining bird(s), so you may have to handle him to one or both of them. If he breaks on the go-bird, he should have marked all three birds satisfactorily.

Remember to wait until the judge calls your number before sending your dog. Of course, you needn't send him immediately thereafter. Look at his head before sending him. If he isn't locked in on the go-bird, pat your leg or do whatever necessary to bring his attention back to the go-bird before sending him.

🐾 Walk-Up Triples

In a walk-up triple, you heel your dog off lead from the holding blind to the starting position set up by the judges. Once there, have your dog sit. Then, tell the judge you're ready. (As a common courtesy, if another dog is honoring, you should first ask his handler whether he's ready.) The judge will tell you to start moving forward. While heeling, don't let your dog get ahead of you, lest he break when the birds go up. Command "Heel!" as often as necessary to keep him by your side. If he forges ahead, don't move faster to keep up with him, for that will only encourage him to forge ahead faster. Instead, command "Heel!" and bring him back to you.

If required to point a gun at each bird, as you probably will be in these tests, put the gun to your shoulder and point it properly. Don't try to cheat by holding the gun casually while you continue watching your dog. In UKC/HRC tests, you're required to fire a popper (blank) shotgun shell at each bird—and they judge gun safety stringently.

When the birdcall or shot that precedes the first memory bird sounds, you may toot the Sit-whistle or command "Sit!" to stop your dog. If he keeps moving, repeat the command. You'll be penalized, perhaps even charged with a controlled break (for which your dog may or may not be dropped, depending on the rules), but at least you might keep him from fully breaking.

After all three birds are down, one of the judges will call your number, after which you can send your dog. With all the excitement, your dog may be confused about which bird to retrieve first. If so, help him focus entirely on the go-bird before you send him.

🐾When to Handle

As mentioned above, after you launch your dog for the go-bird, your job is the same for both types of triples.

The suggestions above (under "Single Marks") on when to handle your dog for a blind retrieve on a mark also apply to triples. As long as your dog is hunting aggressively within the area of the fall, let him hunt. But if he strays outside it for more than a few seconds, stop him and handle him all the way to the bird. If he appears to be about to switch, handle him as quickly as possible, for even the beginning of a switch looks bad to judges. After you've stopped him, handle him to the bird exactly as you would if it were a blind retrieve. (See the instructions in Chapter 8.)

One final point: You can easily get away with handling on one mark in a level 3 hunt test, although your dog will be penalized for failing to mark the bird. You may not be so fortunate if you have to handle him to a second mark during that same hunt test. Most judges look unkindly on any dog that has to be handled on a second mark. After all, this is the highest level, where successful dogs are supposed to be outstanding, especially in marking, which is a hereditary trait. Judges set up triples to determine whether the dogs entered in level 3 can or cannot mark. If you have to handle your dog on two marks, even under the most kindly judges, his work on all other marks and blinds would have to be spectacular for him to qualify.

Clearly, as much as you can, you should "save" your handles for the later birds. In other words, on the first triple of the day, you should hesitate a little longer before handling than you did on the last triple. Of course, if your dog goes clean (no handles) all the way to the last bird of the last triple, and if he has no "black marks" on the blinds, etc., you can safely handle on that bird at the slightest provocation, if you so choose.

🐾The Deliveries

While your dog is returning with the go-bird, you should watch him closely to see which of the two memory birds he would like to retrieve next. As he returns, he'll glance at least once and usually two or three times toward one of the other falls. That's the one most clearly in his thoughts, and therefore the one you should send him for next, unless you have some serious reason to overrule his preference. When you see which way he glances, turn to face that bird, so that when he sits beside you to deliver, he'll be facing his next retrieve.

You should handle the delivery of each bird as described above under "Double Marks." Of course, delivery problems (dropping and picking a bird up, freezing, and so on) are judged more stringently in level 3 than they are in the lower levels.

Selection

In certain situations, your dog may be able to do a better job on a triple if you, rather than he, select the order in which he retrieves the birds. This is called "selection," *which takes lots of training.* Don't spring it on your unsuspecting beastie at a hunt test unless you've prepared him for it very thoroughly in training. Selection comes in two varieties:

1. *Primary selection:* In this, you overrule his natural inclination to retrieve the go-bird first. Instead, you initially send him for one of the memory birds.
2. *Secondary selection:* In this, you allow your dog to retrieve the go-bird first, but then overrule his choice as to which memory bird he should retrieve next.

Obviously, your dog will find secondary selection less disturbing than primary. In secondary selection, he at least gets to follow his instincts for the first retrieve. Here's a situation in which secondary selection might be advantageous: The go-bird is on the outside, say to the left; one memory bird is quite snug with said go-bird while the other is at a wide angle off to the right. If left to his own devices, your dog will retrieve the go-bird first and the outside bird wide on the right second, leaving himself a nasty third retrieve of the snug middle bird. If his memory falters even slightly, he may well return to the go-bird area when sent for this third fall. Thus, if you select that middle memory bird as his second retrieve and overrule his natural tendency to go outside-outside-middle, he will have a better chance of picking up that middle bird cleanly, that is, without being handled. That done, only the much easier memory bird wide to the right will remain.

Here's another, even more common situation in which secondary selection may be advisable: In either a double or triple, a diversion bird is thrown as the dog returns with the next to last bird. If the remaining mark is quite challenging, you might be better off selecting it ahead of the diversion bird. After all, the diversion bird is not a mark, so you won't be penalized for handling your dog to it. However, that last tough memory bird is a mark, and you would be penalized for handling him to it.

Here's a situation in which primary selection might be advantageous: The first memory bird is quite short and right up the middle; the second memory bird is long and to one side; the go-bird is long and to the opposite side. If your dog makes his own decisions, he'll retrieve the long go-bird first, then the long memory bird (outside-outside), and the short middle memory bird last. However, after two long retrieves, he may well overrun the short middle bird and head for the next county, as many dogs do in such a test. However, if you were to primary select and send him for the short middle bird first, after he picks it up, he'll have only the two long and widely separated outside falls to retrieve.

As stated above, selection requires plenty of training. (My book *Retriever Training Drills for Marking*, which is available from the publisher of this book, has an entire chapter on this training.) I would advise anyone wishing to succeed consistently in level 3 hunt tests to train his retriever for selection, both secondary and primary.

Once you've so trained your dog, you should use the following criterion to determine when to select in hunting tests: *Will he be more apt to pick up all the marks without handling if he follows his own instincts about the sequence of retrieves or if I select the sequence for him?* If you're absolutely sure that selection will more likely avoid handling on marks, by all means select! If you have any doubt at all about this, you should probably let your dog make his own sequence decisions. It's that simple.

Diversions

Diversion birds are normally thrown as the dog returns with the next to last retrieve. By the time your dog reaches this level, he won't be much tempted to switch when he sees the diversion bird. However, he will almost certainly want to retrieve it as soon as he delivers the bird he's carrying. If the remaining other mark is relatively simple, you should let him retrieve the diversion next. However, if the remaining bird is a real stem-winder, you may want to select it next and save the diversion for last. Since the diversion is not a mark, you won't be penalized for handling on it, as you would on that last and very difficult mark.

You'll also experience diversion shots, but by now your well-seasoned dog probably won't pay too much attention to them, at least not on marking tests.

🐾 Honoring

Honoring is normally done after the dog completes a set of marks (with or without accompanying blinds). Thus, each dog honors the work of the next dog to run. However, the rules do not require this sequence, so honoring before working is possible.

In a regular triple, after completing the marks (and blinds, if included), the handler heels his dog to the designated honoring position, which is usually several yards to one side or the other of the working dog's position. He and his dog must remain there until released by one of the judges, which normally happens after the working dog is well on his way to the go-bird.

In a walk-up triple, after completing the marks (and blinds, if included), the handler heels his dog to the designated starting point for the honoring dog, which is usually several yards to one side or the other of the working dog's starting position. When the judge so indicates, both handler heel their dogs forward until the birdcall or shot preceding the memory bird sounds, when both handlers may make their dogs sit with either a whistle or a voice command. The honoring dog and his handler must remain there until one of the judges releases them, which normally happens after the working dog is well on his way to the go-bird.

If your honoring dog breaks, command "Heel!" to bring him back lest he and the other dog get into a rumble. He may or may not be dropped, depending on the rules of the format in which you're running him. Of course, if he interferes with the working dog or if you yell loudly enough to disturb the working dog, he should be dropped.

If, while yours is the working dog, the honoring dog breaks but doesn't interfere with your dog, just let your dog keep on going as if nothing has happened. If the honoring dog does interfere with your dog, follow the judge's instructions (which will probably be to pick up your dog and rerun the test later). If the honoring handler's yelling distracts your dog enough so that he stops and looks back at you, you have every right to appeal to the judges for a rerun. However, if they don't grant it, you must do the best you can to get your dog to pick up this set of marks.

Leaving the Line

When you and your dog have completed a triple mark series, which may include blind retrieves and an honor, one of the judges will release you. When he does, exit gracefully and quickly, per the instructions in Chapter 6. Of course, as you leave, don't forget to thank the judges.

Chapter 8
Blind Retrieve Tests

BACKGROUND INFORMATION

What is a Blind Retrieve?

A blind retrieve (called an "unseen" in England) is a retrieve in which the handler directs his dog, by whistle, arm, and voice commands, to a bird the dog has not seen fall. Thus the dog has no idea where the bird is. The handler, of course, must know at least approximately where it is—otherwise, the blind would be leading the blind.

Functionally, a blind retrieve has three distinct "parts": lining, stopping, and casting. First the handler "lines" his dog from his side toward the location of the bird. Then, if the dog drifts off-line as he goes out, the handler stops him with the *Sit*-whistle, which is normally a single whistle blast. On the *Sit*-whistle, the dog should stop, turn to face the handler, sit down, and wait for further directions. After the dog sits thusly, the handler redirects him in the proper direction with an arm signal, usually accompanied by appropriate body English, perhaps, plus a voice or a whistle command.

No dog has any inbred instinct for taking a line, stopping on the Sit-whistle, or taking directional arm casts. Therefore, the trainer must teach the dog everything involved in the blind retrieve. Like all other forms of control training, the trainer does this through a conditioning process that involves repetitive drilling. For more details on this training, see the following of my books (available from the publisher of this book): *Training Retrievers for the Marshes and Meadows, Retriever Training Tests,* and *Retriever Training Drills for Blind Retrieves.*

107

Whence the Blind Retrieve?

Shortly after World War I, Dave Elliot, a young Scottish professional retriever trainer, took a postman's holiday and watched a stock dog trial. There he saw handlers direct their herding dogs with the very whistle and arm signals we now use in blind retrieves. They sent their dogs out beyond the sheep in a "gather," which is similar to our lining. Once the dog was beyond them, the handler stopped him with a Sit-whistle and redirected him with various arm, voice, and whistle commands to guide the dog in herding the sheep as the handler wished. Had Mr. Elliot waited a few years, he would have seen a much different form of stock dog handling, for today's stock dog handlers almost never stop their dogs. Instead they redirect them on the fly with an amazing variety of whistle signals. They no longer use arm signals because that would force the dogs to take their eyes off the animals they're herding. One can only wonder how we would handle our retrievers to blind retrieves if Dave Elliot had first witnessed this more advanced form of stock dog handling.

Mr. Elliot saw the potential for this sort of handling in the English retriever field trials of that period. In those trials, several handlers and their dogs were on the line at the same time. Beaters flushed birds here, there, and everywhere. As each bird was shot, a judge would tell one of the handlers to send his dog to retrieve it. All went well if the dog happened to have seen the bird fall, but if he didn't, he often failed to find it. After such a failure, the judge would instruct another handler to "have a go at it." If the second dog was successful, his handler was said to have "wiped the eye" of the first (unsuccessful) handler. Wiping eyes was a bragging-rights accomplishment that helped win field trials.

Mr. Elliot taught his string of Labradors to respond to the stock dog commands he had observed at that trial. Thereafter, no one wiped his eye, because he could handle his dog to any bird he saw himself, whether or not his dog had marked it. Even more importantly, he began wiping other handlers' eyes with monotonous regularity and thereby became the leading handler in British retriever trials.

In 1931, Jay Carlisle, one of the American economic aristocracy who launched AKC retriever field trials in the early 1930s, brought Dave Elliot to this country to manage his Wingan Kennels and train his

Labradors for hunting and field trial competition. Thus, Dave Elliot was instrumental in building blind retrieves into our trials from the very beginning.

Dave Elliot died on November 7, 1985. Retrieverites throughout the world should always remember him for inventing and promulgating the blind retrieve. *Requiescat in pace.*

HANDLING TECHNIQUES

Basic Setup

Once you've trained your dog to do blind retrieves, if you set him up and launch him properly, he will normally run a very creditable blind. Sure, you may have to handle him a few times to put him on the bird, but you won't have to engage in a tooth-and-toenail battle with him all the way from the line to the bird, as you would if you were to give him a poor start.

Setting up for a blind retrieve. Here the dog is looking away from the picture the handler wants, so the handler says "No" and does not put his hand down.

Setting up for a blind retrieve. Here the dog has the correct picture. To confirm that picture, the handler says "Good" and puts his hand down by the dog's head.

To set him up properly, you need to help him focus his attention on the right "picture." As I've stressed in three different retriever training book (*Training Retrievers for Marshes and Meadows, Retriever Training Tests,* and *Retriever Training Drills for Blind Retrieves,* all available from the publisher of this book), in blind retrieves, a properly trained retriever picks a spot in the scenery before him that his experience tells him should hold the bird, a spot to run to when launched. That spot is his "picture." To find a picture, he flips through his mental "album" of previous blinds and marks until he finds one that matches or nearly matches something he sees before him. Your job as his handler is to help him select a picture that is reasonably close to the location of the bird in the particular blind you and he are facing.

To start off as simply as possible, let's assume that you're setting him up for a "cold" blind, which is a blind run by itself, not in combination with a set of marks. (Thus, a cold water blind is a water blind run without marks, not a blind run in cold water!) Let's also assume that this cold blind includes no visual or aural distractions (like decoys, diversion shots, and so on) and no "poison bird." (Setting up for blinds that include these "added attractions" is covered below.)

The first step in helping your dog select the right picture is to "aim" him in the right direction, that is, to set him up facing the bird in this particular blind. To do this, heel him to the line so that, when he sits, his entire body faces the bird. He should be able to look directly at it without having to turn his head even slightly. His spine should be lined up with the bird. If he sits crooked, move him this way or that (typically with "Here" to move him toward you, and "Heel" to move him away from you) until he's sitting straight. Take your time. You aren't paying the judges by the hour!

Nota bene: In a crosswind, your dog will drift with the wind as he goes toward the blind. The stronger the crosswind and the longer the blind, the more he'll drift. Similarly, in a sidehill blind, he'll drift downhill as he goes. The steeper the hill and the longer the blind, the more he'll drift. To some degree, you can offset this natural drift by giving him a false line into the wind or up the hill. If you guess right, your dog will run a curved (aka "banana") line right to the bird with no further assistance from you. Even if you guess a little too much or not quite enough, he'll probably do a "prettier" job (that is, need fewer whistles) than he would if you were to line him straight at the bird and handle him every time he starts to drift with the wind or down the hill. However, many hunt test judges have been so brainwashed by the necessarily stringent standards of competitive field trials that they tolerate only a small degree of false lining. Rely on your trusty mentor for information about the tolerance level of any specific pair of judges. If he can't help you, play it safe and don't give a false line.

At this point, I can't resist inserting My Frequently Disputed and Often Erroneous Opinion (MFDOEO): When a handler gives his dog a perfect, or even reasonably good false line and the dog "banana-lines" the blind or needs only a check whistle at the end, I feel the two have demonstrated a higher degree of teamwork and mutual understanding than they would have if the handler had lined his dog straight at the bird and then almost wore out his whistle keeping the drifting beast on a tightrope line to the bird. In hunting, which is what hunt tests supposedly simulate, the banana line would be so obviously superior that no discussion would be necessary. If hunt test judges frown on false lining in crosswinds and sidehill blinds, they're showing the influence of field trial standards, not practical hunting requirements. As I've mentioned before, because field trials are competitive and the judges must find a winner from among a large entry of retrievers that are better and better trained every year, field trial judging standards have necessarily become more and more strict over the years. Unfortunately, many judges who participate in both field trials and hunt tests fail to distinguish between the two dog games when judging the latter. Also unfortunately, they often influence other hunt test judges who don't participate in field trials. Of course, my words here won't change this unfortunate situation, but they may at least get a few hunt test participants thinking about this basic injustice. Then, maybe someday....

Enough of MFDOEO. Back to basic setups. Even after your dog is sitting properly, he may not be looking straight ahead. He may glance this way and that. If he does, give him a few seconds to settle down. If he continues to glance around, help him focus on the scenery directly before him by saying "No" whenever he looks away and "Good" whenever he looks straight ahead. Don't use your hand to try to help him focus. If you do, your hand will distract him and keep him from looking for a spot directly ahead of him. Simply veto his bad glances with "No," and confirm his good glances with "Good." You might also pat your leg to turn his head toward you or push your outside knee forward and toward him to turn his head away from you. Eventually, he will settle down and gaze steadily in the direction you're encouraging him to look. We call this steady gaze "locking in." When he locks in properly, you should send him, as explained below under "Launching Your Dog."

Now for a few more complicated setups.

Setting up for Visual Distractions

Judges sometimes employ visual distractions to tempt the dogs to veer off line. For example, until trained otherwise, most dogs find a large white goose decoy placed some distance away from the line to the blind almost irresistible. Ditto for a set of gun standing in plain sight but doing nothing. Sometimes the visual distraction is natural. Once, in a spaniel hunt test water blind, a large white flower was opened toward the line about forty-five degrees off line from the line to the blind. My English Springer, Flick, found it most attractive, and headed for it even after I had "No-ed" him off it rather insistently. But that's why we wear lanyards with whistles, isn't it?

To deal with any visual distraction, first set your dog up for the blind properly. If he stares or even glances repeatedly at the distraction, say "No" each time he looks in the wrong direction. If that doesn't do the trick, re-heel him to face the distraction, and say "NO!" with whatever authority you feel necessary. Then re-heel him back to the correct position and set him up properly again.

Setting up for Combination Marks and Blinds

When a blind is combined with a set of marks, the dog first picks up the marks and then runs the blind. When your dog delivers the last marked bird, before you set him up for the blind, hand the bird to one of the judges. That way, the bird won't distract your dog and you'll have both hands free for handling him on the blind.

For such a blind, the locations of the marks are called "old falls," and dogs not properly trained or handled will return to old falls when sent for a blind. In so doing, the dog is said to "suck back" to the old fall, and old falls are said to tempt the dog with "suction."

Actually, old falls are just another type of visual distraction, so you should deal with them as explained above. Of course, the nearer an old fall is to the line to the blind, the stronger the suction. In an extreme case, it may be all but impossible to get your dog to distinguish between the old fall and the line you are trying to give him. In such a case, you might try giving him a false line *slightly* away from the old fall. If you do, be prepared to stop him and handle him before he gets too far off the true line to the blind. Unlike crosswind and side-hill blinds, in which your drifting dog will curve back naturally to the bird, in this tight old-fall situation, your dog will probably carry the false line straight as an arrow, getting farther and farther off line as he goes. Thus, if you don't stop him rather soon, the judges can legitimately penalize you for "avoiding the test." Your other option is to line him at the blind and then handle him as soon as he begins to suck back to the old fall. This is usually the safer option.

The "under the arc" blind offers a double challenge. The line to the blind goes under the arc of one of the marks. Thus, the old fall is fairly tight on one side and the guns are snug on the other. If either of these distractions bothers your dog, "No" him off it and try setting him up again, and so on. Line him as best you can, and then be ready to handle him as he approaches the arc. Most judges will tolerate it if you have to handle him several times to get him through the slot.

Scent Distractions

Many years ago, field trials went through a fad of putting blinds directly behind old falls. That forced handlers to line their dogs right at old falls and then handle them through the scented area and on to the blind retrieve bird. Happily, that fad faded away and has never come back. I hope no one revives it in hunt tests. But if you run into such a test, simply line your dog at the old fall and then handle him through it, which may take several whistles followed by very hard Back casts.

Field trial judges often use a different type of scent distraction. They will have one of the guns drag a dead bird around in the cover to scent an area upwind of the line to the blind. Then, as the dog goes along on his line to the blind, the scent from that area drifts toward him. Left to his own devices, any sane dog will turn and follow that scent to its source. Thus, the handler must stop his dog and redirect him past the scented area and toward the blind.

In neither of these scent distraction situations can you set your dog up in a way that will help him when he hits the scent. You simply have to set him up for the blind as if the hazard didn't exist and then handle him through it when he gets there.

Setting up for Double Blinds

In a double blind, the first bird picked up becomes something akin to an old fall for the second blind, in that a dog, when sent for the second blind, might want to return to the spot where he picked up the first one. Deal with this just as you would an old fall or any other visual distraction.

After your dog delivers the first bird, you should hand it to one of the judges before starting to set up for the second blind. That way, you won't have a bird in your hand to distract your dog, and you'll have both hands free for handling him on the second blind.

Setting up for Diversion Shots

If the diversion shot occurs before you send your dog for the blind, treat it as you would an old fall or visible distraction, even if the gun isn't visible. If the diversion shot occurs after you launch your dog, be prepared to handle him as soon as he veers off toward the sound.

Setting up for Diversion Birds

A diversion bird is thrown as the dog returns with the blind retrieve bird and tempts the dog to switch. The closer it's thrown to the dog's path, the more tempting it is. The "bulldog," which is thrown directly in the dog's path and fairly close to him, is the worst-case scenario. However, if you've trained your dog thoroughly, he should sail right through diversion birds. Nevertheless, have your whistle in your mouth, just in case.

Remember that diversion birds are not marks, so you can handle your dog to them without being charged for handling on a mark.

Setting up for Poison Birds

A poison bird is a mark thrown just before you send your dog on a blind retrieve. The dog must mark this diversion bird, but he cannot retrieve it until after he has completed the blind. If he picks up the diversion bird before getting the blind, he fails the test. In a sense, the diversion bird is "poison" for the dog until after he completes the blind, which is why we call it a "poison bird." Naturally, the closer the poison bird falls to the line to the blind, the more tempting it is.

When you go to the line, set your dog up facing the poison bird station. Let him watch the bird's arc closely, so he can mark it. Then say "No" and re-heel him to face the line to the blind. If he glances (or stares) at the poison bird area, treat it just as you would a visual distraction.

Nota bene: Unlike a diversion bird, a poison bird is indeed a mark, so you'll be penalized if you have to handle your dog to it. Since he must remember it while running the blind, you should make sure he marks it well before you set him up for the blind.

Setting up for Water Blinds

Setting up for a water blind is pretty much the same as setting up for a similar land blind. However, if the water blind has an angled entry, you might want to set your dog up a little "fat," that is, give him a slightly false line that increases the entry angle. Don't overdo it, of course, lest you be penalized for avoiding the test.

Launching Your Dog

Watch your dog's head to determine what picture he has. As soon as he "locks in" on a reasonable approximation of the right one, say

The arm signal for a straight "Back" cast.

The arm signal for a straight "Over" cast.

"Good," to reassure him, and then launch him! If you dillydally around after he's firm on the right picture, he'll become unsure and may start glancing around for another picture. While judging, I've seen many handlers blow a blind retrieve before they ever launched their dogs simply by not saying "Back!" when their dogs were all set to go. In many such cases, the dog began glancing this way and that again. Then the handler panicked and launched the poor beast when he no longer had any picture at all! Typically the dog ran off in some arbitrary direction for a short distance, perhaps popping or wobbling this way and that until the handler finally blew the Sit-whistle. From there it was hack, hack, hack, all the way to the bird.

When your dog locks in on a good picture, reassure him with "Good" and then send him. He who hesitates here may not be totally lost, but he'll usually louse up a blind unnecessarily.

🐾 The "Fairway" for Blind Retrieves

After launching your dog toward the blind, you need to know when to intervene (stop and redirect him) and when to let him continue on his current path. Concerning this critical decision, I'll offer some common sense and logic, after which I'll explain why common sense and logic often have nothing to do with it.

First, the common sense and logic. No dog can run an absolutely straight or tightrope line to every blind retrieve. First off, his handler may not set him up exactly right. Second, as he goes out, the terrain, wind, and other hazards along the way can take him off line, at least a little. Thus, we must allow the dog a certain amount of leeway on the way to the bird. Borrowing a golf term, I call this allowable leeway the "fairway." As long as the dog is moving toward the bird and remains within that fairway, his handler should let him run, and should not handle him with whistle and arm signals. However, if the dog drifts out of that fairway, his handler should toot the *Sit*-whistle and wave a helping arm at his errant animal.

Common sense and logic certainly suggest that the fairway should be quite narrow near the line and should gradually widen as it goes toward the bird, reaching its greatest width right at the bird. How wide should it be at the bird? Common sense and logic suggest that it should be the same width as the area of the fall would be if this were a single mark or the go-bird of a multiple mark instead of a blind retrieve. If the dog has that much leeway in a mark, why would he have any less on a blind? Thus, for a 100-yard blind, common sense and logic dictate that the fairway should be twenty yards wide at the bird, and so on.

Using this rule of thumb, you can estimate an appropriate fairway for any blind by estimating how wide the area of the fall would be if it were a single mark or go-bird. Further, in a crosswind or sidehill blind, you could approximate a curved fairway that would allow you to give your dog a reasonable false line into the wind or up the hill.

So much for common sense and logic. Now for some reality that defies said common sense and logic. As mentioned before, many hunt test judges are also field trialers who are strongly influenced by field trial standards, especially for blind retrieves. Since field trials are competitive, and since the straightest line to a blind is the best job, field trialers generally feel that it's better to use many whistles to keep your dog on a precise line to the bird than it is to let him run somewhat off line and then handle him near the bird. Of course, they should not expect that in hunt tests, which are noncompetitive. In hunt tests, as

The arm signal and body English for a straight "Come" cast.

long as a dog stays within a reasonable fairway, he shouldn't be bothered with Sit-whistles. However, hunt test judges who suffer field-trial tunnel vision expect handlers to keep their dogs on a precise line to the bird, even if that means hacking the poor beast all the way, which *jest ain't purty,* folks! Tweeet! *(angled) Back!* Tweeet! *(angled) Back!* Tweeet! *(angled) Back!* And so on, until either the dog reaches the bird or the handler wears out both of his whistles.

Such judges, when giving their pre-test dog instructions, usually tell the handlers that they expect precise lines. They may spell it out that way, saying they prefer many whistles on a straight line to fewer whistles on a slightly angled line. But more often they use code expressions, like "Challenge the blind! Challenge the blind!" (often uttered in enthusiastic but insistent duplication). If you run under such a judge, forget common sense and logic. Give your whistle as much of a workout as is required to keep your long-suffering retriever on a tightrope line all the way to the bird.

After the Sit-Whistle

Okay, you've launched your dog and he has run straight for some distance. But then he veers off line and leaves the fairway, so you blow the *Sit*-whistle. He's sitting there facing you, waiting for you in your

The arm signal for an angled "Back" cast.

The arm signal for an angled "Come" cast.

great wisdom to re-direct him to the bird. Incidentally, if he's sitting there but not looking at you, you should toot the *Sit*-whistle again (and again, if necessary) to get him to gaze intently in your direction. Don't try to handle him when he's ignoring you! Okay, now that he's looking your way steadily, what should you do next?

First off, please remember that you're participating in a noncompetitive hunt test, not a competitive field trial. Why is this so important? Because field trialers, in order to win, must take chances that make no sense for hunt testers. For example, a principle of field trial success states that, other things being equal, the fewer the whistles, the better the job. Actually, this really means the fewer the casts the better the job, but since a *Sit*-whistle precedes every cast, field trial jargon has associated this pearl of wisdom with the number of *Sit*-whistles it takes to get the dog to the bird. Therefore, if you were running in a field trial and your dog was sitting ten yards off the line to the bird and forty yards short of it, you would be wise to give him an angled *Back* cast instead of a ten-yard *Over* followed by a forty-yard *Back*. Either will work, of course, but the angled cast uses only one whistle, whereas the *Over* and *Back* combination requires two whistles. When angled casts were first introduced into the field trial world, they were said to "roll two whistles into one." Not surprisingly then, at a field trial, you'll see many, many angled casts, and very few straight *Overs*, except right near the bird.

However, to succeed in a hunt test, you don't have to beat any of the other participants. You simply have to pick up the meat in an acceptable way. Thus, if your dog will more likely respond correctly to a straight *Over* followed by a straight *Back* (or *Come*-whistle) than he would to an angled *Back* (or angled *Come*-whistle), you'd be most foolish to risk the angled cast. Gambling that way gains you nothing and could cost you one or more cast refusals. Actually, under most circumstances, the pair of straight casts (*Over/Back* or *Over/Come*) is safer, because the straight *Over* more clearly redirects your dog away from his errant way than would an angled *Back* (or angled *Come*). In fact, hunt test clubs would probably pass out more qualifying rosettes if all angled casts were outlawed in these events. I'm not advocating such a radical measure, for sometimes angled casts do make sense, but more often than not a pair of straight casts will serve the typical hunt test handler better.

For hunt testers, giving proper casts need not be the complex science it has become in the field trial world, where they've developed what I call "handler ballet" through the introduction of various subtle combinations of body language and arm signals, such as stepping lightly to the left while giving a vigorous right-arm *Back*, and who knows what all else. However, there are a few basic principles you should employ in getting your dog to the bird with as few cast refusals as possible.

For example, when giving a *Back* cast after an *Over*, you should normally change arms. A left-arm *Back* should follow a right-arm *Over* and vice versa. If you give both casts with the same arm, your dog may well continue the *Over* instead of taking the *Back*.

Then, too, there's the difference between a "hard" and a "soft" *Over*. In giving a hard *Over*, you step rapidly in the direction of the cast, as you shout "Over!" and pump your arm vigorously. In that case, your dog will most likely scallop back instead of taking your *Over*. Sometimes that's exactly what you want, but not normally. In giving a soft *Over*, you step slowly, speak softly, and pump your arm slowly. In that case, your dog will be more inclined to take and carry your *Over*, which is normally what you want. In a critical situation, you might give it even more softly, that is, by pumping your arm very slowly without stepping or speaking at all. In a very critical situation, one in which experience tells you that your dog is determined to turn and go back instead of taking your *Over*, you can "trick" him into complying with your wishes by standing still and pumping your arm slowly while tooting the *Come*-whistle. The *Come*-whistle will startle him enough to neutralize his determination to go *Back*. Then, seeing you wave your arm in an *Over* cast, he may question your sanity, but he'll almost certainly take your *Over* cast very politely. *But save that little gimmick for real emergencies.* Never use it in training and don't use it even in hunt tests unless you feel nothing else would work. If you use it too often, you'll lose the element of surprise, which is what makes it work.

You can also use hard and soft *Back* casts. The louder you shout "Back!" and the more vigorously you give the cast with your arm, the more powerfully you will drive your dog to the rear. Thus, when he's still a long way from the bird, you should give a hard *Back*. However, when he's close to the bird and you fear a hard *Back* might make him race straight past it, give a soft *Back*, in which you say "Back" softly or not at all and raise your arm slowly.

One final warning: When your dog seems to have found the bird and sticks his head down into the cover to pick it up, refrain from blowing the *Come*-whistle until you see the bird in his mouth. I once saw a man blow the *Come*-whistle too soon, which caused his overly obedient dog to start in without the bird. Apparently the bird wasn't exactly where the handler thought it was, and his dog stuck his head down into the cover for some other reason. Then, hearing the *Come*-whistle, he stopped hunting and headed back to the boss, as ordered. So the man had to start handling him to the bird all over again.

After the Delivery

After your dog has delivered the bird to you, you should hand it to one of the judges and do whatever is expected of you next, whether that is to pick up the poison bird, to honor, or to leave the line. As you exit, remember to thank the judges.

Chapter 9
Other Types of Tests

BACKGROUND INFORMATION

Initially, in addition to the various non-slip retriever tests (marks and blinds), all four formats included an upland hunting test at certain levels, and three formats (AKC, UKC/HRC, and NAHRA) included a trailing or tracking test.

In the trailing or tracking tests, the judges had a bird (usually alive, but sometimes dead) dragged through cover for a reasonable distance, say fifty to seventy-five yards, with one or two turns along the way. Then the handler brought his dog to the start of the "track" and encouraged him to follow it and find the bird. Of course, a birdy dog with a decent nose will track crippled birds quite naturally without any training. The trick in this type of tracking test has always been to communicate to the dog that the drag scent is a track and that the boss wants him to follow it. Thus, passing one of these trailing tests does require some sort of training.

In the upland hunting tests, the dog must range out ahead of the handler and hunt for planted birds, while staying within easy gun range all the time. Quartering has never been a requirement. The dog need only "hunt to the gun," as any decent retriever will do with a modicum of training.

AKC dropped both of these tests a few years after the beginning of their program. Currently UKC/HRC still carries them as options in level 2, while NAHRA requires them in both level 2 and level 3. CKC requires an upland hunting test in level 3. For specific requirements, consult the appropriate rule book.

UKC/HRC also has a separate program for upland hunting, for which they offer separate hunts. Dogs that qualify in these a certain number of times earn the title "Upland Hunter" (UH). Here, too, you should consult the rule book for specific requirements.

The following presentation offers general instructions for handling your dog in these types of tests.

TESTS WITHIN THE REGULAR FORMATS

Trailing Tests

In this type of test, someone drags a bird through cover for a reasonable distance. The path of the dragged bird normally includes at least one turn. As long as the dog finds the bird, it doesn't matter whether he tracks it or quarters the area and picks up the bird's scent that way.

If you want your dog to track the bird, you must establish some way of indicating your wishes to your dog in training. You might squat down, point to the ground near the location of the start of the trail, and say, "Hunt dead" (or some similar expression). But whatever you do to tell him to trail, he must be able to distinguish it from your other commands.

Once, when judging one of the early AKC hunt tests, I watched a handler set his dog up for trailing with his blind retrieve sequence ("Dead bird...Line...Back"). The dog failed the test by taking off on a very nice line, which he carried for about seventy-five yards before the handler realized that his pooch wasn't trailing. The dog failed the test because the handler didn't ever let him know what he was supposed to do. As the handler left the line shaking his head, he commented that he just couldn't understand why his dog hadn't stuck his nose down and started trailing.

"How do you set him up for a blind retrieve?" I asked.

"Well, I say, 'Dead bird....' Oh, my golly!" he said. "It was all my fault, wasn't it?"

"Yup," I said. "Better luck next time. You have a nice dog there." When you start a trailing test, make sure your dog knows what game you're asking him to play.

🐾 Upland Test

This is a test in which the dog is expected to hunt ahead of the handler much as he would in hunting upland game birds. Quartering is not required, but the dog should stay well within gun range and should give every indication that he is actually hunting.

The requirements vary widely from format to format and level to level. The dog may or may not be required to find and flush a bird. If this is not required, he may be required to find and retrieve a dead bird or to witness a bird released ahead of him either by hand or from a remote release trap. If he is required to find and flush a bird, he may or may not be required to be steady, and so on. Read the rules currently in force in your chosen format to determine how to train your dog for this type of test. If you feel he's ready, just handle him in the test as you do in training and actual hunting. Be especially careful to keep him within easy gun range, for some judges are very picky about how far ahead the dog should be allowed to range.

THE UKC/HRC UPLAND HUNT PROGRAM

In these tests, the dog must hunt within gun range, find and flush a bird, remain steady to wing, shot, and kill, and then retrieve the shot bird. In other words, it's just like a real upland hunting experience. In unusual conditions, the requirement for a flush may be waived, and a bird may be launched by hand or from a remote release trap just ahead of the dog. A walk-up and a trailing test may be incorporated into the test.

If your dog is ready for this advanced type of upland hunting, you should handle him just as you would in training or actual hunting. Of course, the hunt test environment may pump him up and make him more difficult to control. If so, rely on two whistle commands (the *Sit*-whistle and the *Come*-whistle) to keep him within reasonable range of you as he hunts. If he pushes out too far ahead of you, stop him with the *Sit*-whistle and make him wait for you to catch up. If he swings too far to either side, bring him back toward you with the *Come*-whistle, and then release him to hunt (with *Okay*, or whatever you use) as soon as he's within your comfort zone again.

When the bird goes up, blow the *Sit*-whistle with all the authority you can muster. If he's slow to sit, blow it again. To qualify, he must
stop.

The retrieves in these upland tests should be quite simple compared to those in regular marking tests. Even so, be ready to handle
him to the bird if he gets lost and starts disturbing too much cover.
Other birds may be planted in the field, and if he flushes one of them
out of gun range, he perpetrates a big no-no.

QUARTERING

Not Necessary, but Nice

None of the retriever hunt test formats that include upland hunting tests require quartering. In fact, the rules of each one specifically
state that quartering is not required. Thus, you needn't train your dog
to windshield-wiper back and forth in front of you like a spaniel in
order to qualify in any of these tests.

However, the very fact that the rules state that quartering is not
necessary suggests that it is highly desirable. Actually, quartering is the
most efficient and productive way for a flushing dog to hunt the types
of upland cover that game birds, especially pheasants, seem to prefer,
like draws, C.P.R. ground, and so forth. Quartering such areas allows
the dog to locate all the birds with a minimum of time and effort, all
the while staying well within gun range. The quartering dog sweeps
back and forth about fifteen yards in front of his handler. Each cast
takes him about twenty yards to one side or the other of the handler.
Thus, he covers a succession of forty-yard swaths to the front without
ever getting more than about twenty-five yards from the boss. Such a
pattern allows the dog to find and flush any bird in the entire
"shootable" area ahead of his handler. What could be more productive?

Of course, if you and your dog seldom hunt in the uplands, and
your primary goal here is to pass one of these retriever upland hunting tests, you shouldn't waste your time training him to quarter. He
can pass simply by hunting ahead of you in any reasonable manner.

However, if you and he do a lot of upland hunting, you'll almost certainly benefit greatly from training him to quarter. It will be not only time and effort well spent, but also lots of fun.

✋ Go and See for Yourself

If you'd like to witness "flat-pattern" quartering at its finest, you should attend an AKC hunting test or field trial for spaniels. You'll enjoy it. You'll learn plenty. And, I promise you, you won't come away contaminated in any way by this exposure to humans and canines outside of the retriever fold! For reasons I've never understood, many fanciers of each of the three classifications of sporting dogs (retrievers, spaniels, and pointing breeds) confine their activities exclusively to those of their own breed's classification, and seem to take a strange pride in knowing as little as possible about the talents of the other two classifications. They seem to feel that any acknowledgement of these talents would constitute some heinous and unforgivable form of disloyalty. Actually, every trainer, regardless of his breed preference, can learn valuable lessons from those who train breeds of the other classifications. For example, retriever pro Dave Elliot invented the blind retrieve after attending a stock dog field trial. Granted, after visiting a spaniel event, you probably won't make a similarly monumental contribution to the retriever world. But you'll almost certainly become a better retriever trainer. To locate spaniel hunting tests and field trials in your area, check the AKC website, listed in the Appendix.

At these spaniel events, you'll see quartering that will almost take your breath away. The dog swishes rapidly to the left, and then swishes back rapidly to the right. So fast! So animated and stylish! And so productive! You'll see these spaniels make flashy, crashing fly-or-die flushes that give even the most athletic pheasants no chance to run. In the more advanced levels, you'll see steadiness to wing, shot, and kill that will amaze you. As the bird flushes, the spaniel may well leap high in the air after it (and sometimes actually catch the bird!). Then the dog comes back down to earth in a sitting position, and remains there until sent to retrieve. The dog may quiver with excitement, but he won't move. You'll see retrieves that, although not as long and complicated as those in retriever events, are quite impressive, especially when the dog has to trail a crippled bird for a considerable distance. Fleet-footed cripples are fairly common in spaniel trials and tests, primarily because the gunners ride the birds out as far as possible in order to give the dogs long and challenging retrieves.

A final reassurance: After attending a spaniel event, or even several spaniel events, you'll still be a faithful and unsullied retrieverite, acceptable in the purest of retriever circles. But, you'll have had your eyes opened to vast new training possibilities.

Training for Quartering

If you decide that you should train your retriever to quarter and would like more information on how to go about it, read my book *HUP! Training Flushing Spaniels the American Way* (available from the publisher of this book). Although intended for spaniel trainers, the training techniques in this book work just as well with retrievers.

Training a dog to quarter is lots of fun. While you quarter your dog, a couple of your buddies walk along in a line with you. One is about twenty yards to your left, while the other is about twenty yards to your right, just like in upland hunting. Their job is to shoot the birds your dog flushes, thereby allowing you to concentrate on handling him, not on shooting birds. Later, while your buddies take turns quartering their dogs, you'll walk along on one side or the other, shooting flushed birds for their dogs. In other words, in this training, there are only two jobs: handling your own dog, or shooting flushed birds for your buddies' dogs. What a picnic! You won't have to throw marks; you won't have to pop; you won't have to plant blinds; in fact, you won't have to do any of the more onerous jobs we all do in training retrievers for marks and blinds. Thus, for retriever trainers, teaching dogs to quarter becomes an exhilarating vacation. Try it!

SECTION III

Addenda

Chapter 10

Putting on a Hunt Test

Since you and your dog benefit so much from the efforts of the members of clubs that put on hunt tests, you should learn more about what those members must do to provide you with these opportunities. Let's skip past the challenging process of gaining approval from one of the sponsoring organizations (AKC, UKC/HRC, NAHRA, or CKC) to conduct "official" hunt tests under the rules of said sponsoring organization. Let's assume that has all been done and that the club conducts hunt tests regularly. This being the case, the first step the club must take for each hunt test is to name a hunt test committee. Most clubs do this about twelve months before the anticipated hunt test date.

HUNT TEST COMMITTEE

This committee usually consists of a chair, a secretary, and three to five other members. They must do the following jobs long before the hunt test begins:

1. Coordinate the hunt test dates with the sponsoring organization (AKC, UKC/HRC, NAHRA, or CKC).
2. Select a site for the hunt test and coordinate permission from the landowner.
3. Select a panel of judges, and get each judge's agreement to judge the specific testing level on the specific date. The committee must plan the necessary transportation, lodgings, and so forth for each judge.
4. Select marshals for each testing level.
5. Select a captain of the guns for the entire hunt test.
6. Make arrangements with a bird supplier to have a sufficient

number of birds available at the site on the days of the hunt test.

7. Make arrangement for lunches for the judges and workers during the hunt test.
8. Make arrangements for lunches for the handlers at the test site, if that is the practice.
9. Check on area motels to see which will accept dogs, and include this information with the entry forms.
10. Procure a supply of qualifying rosettes.
11. Procure appropriate gifts for the judges.
12. Arrange to have directional signs available to help people find the site.
13. Make arrangements for the submission of entries, whether on-line or by paper entry forms.
14. Arrange for all the equipment (holding blinds, launchers, radios, and so forth) needed for the hunt test.
15. Establish a closing date for entries.
16. Promulgate information about the test and mail entry forms to interested or potentially interested people.
17. Receive all entries and confirm receipt when that is requested.

On the closing date, the committee must do the following:

1. Sort the entries by testing level.
2. Hold a drawing for each testing level to determine the running order of the entered dogs.
3. Prepare a program listing all dogs in each testing level in running order.
4. Prepare the official judges' books.
5. List the running order of each level on-line.
6. Inform by mail those who have sent stamped envelopes and asked what their numbers will be.

On the day before the hunt test, the committee must do the following:

1. Meet the incoming judges, get them to their lodgings, and arrange for their meals.

2. Take the judges to the test site and help them set up their tests. This includes having appropriate equipment, manpower, and setup dogs available.
3. Identify the equipment needs for each set of judges and make arrangements for it to be available for the hunt test.
4. Identify appropriate test dogs for each testing level.

During the hunt test, the committee must do the following:

1. Arrive early and stay all day every day.
2. Put out directional signs to help people find the test site.
3. Make sure all the equipment needed and a good supply of birds is in place for each test in each testing level.
4. Assist the marshal of each testing level in assigning competent help for each test.
5. Assist the marshal in rotating the helpers at each testing level so no one is overworked.
6. Assist the marshal in getting lunches, etc., for the judges and helpers at each testing level.
7. Handle all complaints and disagreements other than those that fall under the jurisdiction of the judges. The committee acts as the trial board should a formal misconduct charge be made.
8. Assist the marshals in disposing of dead birds and in any other way necessary throughout the days of the hunt test.

After the hunt test, the committee must do the following:

1. Make sure the test site is properly cleaned and that all equipment is properly stored.
2. Assist the judges in getting to the airport for their return flights.
3. Fill out all paperwork required by the sponsoring organization (AKC, UKC/HRC, NAHRA, or CKC) and return it promptly.
4. Submit all payable bills to the club treasurer for payment.
5. Prepare a financial report for the club officers and any other hunt test reports they request.
6. Make recommendations to the club officers for improvements the club might make in future hunt tests.

As you can see, the hunt test committee is a very busy group of people. (And I must admit, I've probably omitted some of their chores and understated others.) Here's anecdotal evidence of the importance of this committee in the eyes of the sponsoring organizations: At one AKC hunting test, in the middle of the afternoon, the hunt test committee chairman said that since everything was running smoothly, he was going to go home to take a nap; the AKC representative overheard this and said, "If you leave, I'll shut down the entire hunting test until you get back here!" Naturally, he stayed.

HUNT TEST JOBS

Each hunt test requires a large "cast of characters" all day, every day. Of course, each testing level requires two judges, for a total of six or eight judges. Some of these may not be, and usually aren't, club members; at least some will be "imports" from other clubs, perhaps even other parts of the country. However, club members normally fill all the other positions necessary for a successful hunt test. To help you appreciate the total effort of the test-giving club, here's a list of the jobs that must be done.

Three key players in every testing level: two judges (with books) and a marshal (with clipboard).

Marshals

Each testing level has a marshal whose job, in a nutshell, is to do everything necessary to allow the judges to concentrate on judging. On setup day (normally the day before the hunt test) he accompanies his set of judges to the test site, gives them an overview of it, and answers their questions. He brings along all the equipment necessary to set up and try out a test. That, of course, includes bird throwers and an appropriate setup dog. He writes down everything the judges will need for each test, so he can make sure it's all there when they need it.

On the day of the test, before each series, he summons the handlers to the line en masse for the judges' instructions. He then makes a suitable test dog available for the judges. He (or an assistant) checks the handlers and their dogs in, so that he can call them to the line in their proper running order. He notes scratches, no-shows, and dogs that must run out of sequence because they or their handlers are also entered in other testing levels. He schedules reruns for dogs the judges want to rerun for any reason.

After the test dog runs, the marshal calls each dog to the line in the proper order and announces its numbers to the judges. He tells the blind planters when to plant the blinds (and then watches to make sure they do so!). Before each dog comes to the line, he calls "Guns up!" to alert the shooters and throwers. He takes the retrieved birds from the judges, hangs the good ones on the drying rack and disposes of those unfit for further use. He fills containers with usable birds and has runners take them out to the various gunning and blind planting stations as needed. He schedules and provides relief for each worker.

Between series he gets the callback list from the judges and announces the number of the dogs called back for the handlers. Then he leads the handler to the location of the next series. At the end of the last series of the testing level, he leads the handlers to the place where the qualifying rosettes are to be awarded. After getting the list of qualifying dogs, he awards the rosettes to the handler, usually after making a little speech complimenting the judges, the workers, the handlers, and the dogs.

Clearly, the marshal is the very backbone of each testing level, and I must admit I've probably omitted some of his chores and understated others.

Captain of the Guns

The captain of the guns chooses the live guns for the entire hunt test and schedules them appropriately for each testing level. He, of course, must select excellent shots who are absolutely safe in their gun handling practices.

It rarely happens, but if a set of guns seems to be having an off day, the judges will ask the marshal to have them replaced. Then the marshal will ask the captain of the guns to send another set of guns to the testing level in question.

I've only judged one hunt test in which we had problems with the live guns. In a water test, the live ducks weren't strong fliers, so every time the guns missed a bird, it came down somewhere out there in that quite large pond. Before we could get on with the test, someone had to sluice the duck and then send a pick-up dog to make a sometimes long swim to retrieve it. This took up lots of time. Changing guns didn't help, for apparently no one in that club could shoot any better than I can, which *jest ain't good enough* to be a live gun at a hunt test. We spent so much time dealing with missed ducks that we had to continue our tests the next day. However, in most hunt tests, the live guns are such outstanding shots that a person might hardly notice them (unless said person is a mediocre shot like me!).

Live Guns

Whenever the judges set up a test that includes a shot flier, they need a pair of gunners who are both highly skilled and safety-conscious. Why two? Because, human beings being so predictably human, a single gunner might miss too often. The selected gunners should know where the judges want the bird dropped and concentrate on doing exactly that. Above all, they should *never* get into competition with one another to see who can shoot each bird first.

A set of live guns ready to shoot a flier.

Normally, the two live guns and the live thrower sit in chairs, with a stack of bird crates behind them. When the marshal says, "Guns up!" all three stand. As the thrower readies the bird, the two live guns load their shotguns (which should otherwise be empty) and prepare to shoot. They concentrate on the spot in the sky where they must hit the bird so it will fall where the judges want it to fall. When the live thrower blows his duck call or says "Bird," the live guns prepare themselves for the launching of the bird. If all goes well, they let the bird get to the desired spot and then shoot it.

However, several other things can happen. First, the bird may fly in an unsafe direction, like toward the line where the handler, dog, judges, and gallery are located, or toward another gunning station, or toward the blind planter. In any such case, the guns should call, "Safety!" and "unshoulder" their shotguns. Second, the bird may not fly very well, but instead drop down a few yards in front of them. In that case, everyone involved should follow the judges' instructions for recovering the bird. Third, the bird may fly in a safe but wrong direction, like straight behind the live guns. In that case, they should shoot or not shoot according to the direction of the judges. If they shoot such a bird, all hands should then follow the judges' directions for recovering it.

Incidentally, the best group of live guns I ever saw shot at the hunt test I judged the weekend after the one with the disastrous shooting mentioned above. Because of that recent bad experience, I came to the site more than a little gun-shy (awful pun!). When I saw these three people, I mistook them for spectators. Actually, they looked very "indoorsy," like three bridge players just passing by, perhaps needing directions to a nearby tournament. When one of them told me they were to be our live gunners, I almost had a heart attack. One man was tall, heavy, and moved awkwardly. The second was his wife, who was petite, blonde, and vivacious. The third was his brother, who was an average-looking guy. None of them looked like they had ever been off the pavement in their lives. To my great relief, I learned that the lady was a state skeet-shooting champion, her husband made his living shooting live pigeons in Mexico, and the brother had a similar background. They shot very fancy shotguns, and believe me, they never missed. They took turns shooting in pairs, but any one of them would have done as well all alone. They dropped every bird exactly where we asked them to drop it. I was never so glad to be wrong in all my life.

🐾 Live Throwers

Whenever the judges set up a test that includes a shot flier, that is, a bird that is thrown live and shot in flight, they need a live thrower to throw the bird. Some clubs use mechanical bird throwers, while others rely on hand-thrown fliers. Hand-throwing a bird so that it flies vigorously in the proper direction takes experience, so good live throwers can be difficult for a club to locate.

The thrower and the two live guns normally sit in chairs, with a stack of bird crates full of live birds behind them. When the marshal says, "Guns up!" all three stand. The thrower takes a bird from a bird crate, readies it for launching (by a mechanical device or by hand), and watches the judges for the signal to throw. When he sees the judge's signal, he may or may not first have to blow a duck call before throwing the bird. Either way, immediately before launching the bird, he says, "Bird!" to alert the live guns that he's about to put the bird in the air. Then he launches it.

If all goes well and the guns drop the bird in an acceptable spot, the thrower and guns sit down and remain quiet while the dog works. However, a number of unacceptable situations can and often do occur. First, the bird may fly away unharmed. In that case, the judges call, "No bird," allow the dog to rerun the test later, and start the test over for the next dog. Second, a lightly hit bird may come down far from the intended spot, but in a place that could interfere with a dog's work. In that case, the judges call, "No bird," allow the dog to rerun the test later, and take whatever steps necessary to have the crippled bird caught and removed from the area before running the next dog. Third, a well-hit bird may fall in a place unacceptable to the judges. In that case, the judges call, "No bird," allow the dog to rerun later, have the bird picked up and removed from the area, and start the test over with the next dog. In all such eventualities, the live thrower should follow any instructions the judges give him.

Control Bird Throwers

The thrower for each control bird station in a marking test throws a dead bird for each dog according to the judges' instructions. He and his associated popper normally sit in chairs except when actually popping and throwing. To get consistent throws, some clubs have their throwers use mechanical bird launchers, while others have their throwers hand-throw the birds.

When the marshal says, "Guns up!" the thrower takes a bird from his container of birds and stands up. If he is using a mechanical thrower, he loads the bird into it. If not, he simply prepares to hand-throw it. In fairness to the dog, he should select only birds in good condition. He should also set any bad birds he finds in his container aside so he can later show them to the marshal, who will dispose of them properly. After the popper shoots or blows his duck call, the thrower launches the bird (mechanically or by hand) according to the judges' instructions. To give all dogs the same test, he should make each throw as much like all the others as he can. After making the throw, the thrower and the popper sit down and remain quiet while the dog works.

Many years ago, I judged a hunt test for a club that hired the local high school football team to act as control bird throwers. Great idea! However, in this case it didn't work out as planned. The night before the first day of the hunt test, that football team had lost a heart-breaker to a rival school. You never saw such a group of aching and

A control bird station, with the thrower on the left and the popper on the right. The popper is ready to blow a duck call, as is often required.

depressed young athletes! They did the best they could, but we had to relieve most of them in order to get decent throws for the dogs. Not every great idea pans out.

If the judges call a no-bird, they will tell the throwers to pick up the birds they have thrown. Then they start the entire test over. In such a case, the thrower should retrieve the bird he threw as quickly as possible.

If a dog cannot find the bird, the judges may ask the thrower to help the dog out. If so, the thrower should do whatever the judges may have told him to do in such a case. Lacking any such instructions, he should walk out, pick up the bird, attract the dog's attention and then drop it again as the dog approaches.

Before the test dog runs, the judges may have the thrower launch several birds in order to scent the area of the fall. This equalizes the test for the early dogs that would otherwise have to hunt an area with less scent than would the later dogs. After tossing these birds, the thrower should be sure to pick up every one he threw.

🦆 Poppers

A "popper" is a person who fires a blank shell from a shotgun as part of a test. Sometimes he also blows a duck call. Judges need poppers for control birds in marking tests and for diversion shots. Some clubs mount the popper's shotgun on a little stand while others expect the poppers to hand-hold it.

Each control bird station in a marking test has a popper and a control bird thrower. Normally, they sit in chairs except when actually popping and throwing. When the marshal says, "Guns up!" the two stand up and the popper watches the judge. When the judge signals, the popper fires his gun (or blows his duck call). Then the bird thrower launches the bird. When the bird reaches the high point of its arc, the popper fires his gun in the direction of the bird. Then, the two sit down and wait quietly while the dog works.

If a control bird is used as a diversion bird, the popper's job is basically the same, except that the judge signals to him while a dog is working rather than before the dog leaves the line.

The station for each diversion shot requires a popper. He normally sits in a chair except when actually popping. When the marshal says, "Guns up!" he stands and looks at the judge. When the judge signals, he shoots his gun and then sits down again. He should remain silent and motionless while each dog works.

₪ Blind Planters

Whenever the judges set up a series that includes a blind retrieve, they need someone to put a bird down in the place they designate for said blind retrieve. That person is called the "blind planter." If a series includes two blinds, it may require one or two blind planters, depending on the location of the two blinds.

The judges will select a place in which the blind planter should hide whenever he is not actually planting a bird. Normally that hiding place is forty or fifty yards farther from the line than the planted bird. That way, the dog should never encounter the blind planter while doing the blind retrieve.

Before the test dog runs, the marshal will give the blind planter a container (sack, bucket, whatever) full of dead birds and indicate where he is to hide. The blind planter then walks to his designated hiding place, carrying his container of dead birds. To avoid laying

A blind planter's job involves lots of idle time, and he can't even watch the dogs work. Thus, as Isaac Taylor shows here, it's a good idea to take a book along to read during the sometimes long intervals between the times when the marshal hollers, "Plant the blind!"

down a scent trail that dogs might follow, as he walks he holds the container of birds high enough so it doesn't contact the ground or cover. Once in his hiding place, he puts the container of birds down and sits down in his chair. If the club uses walkie-talkie type radios for communications, the blind planter will have one, so that the marshal can tell him when to plant a blind. If the club doesn't use these radios, the marshal shouts, "Plant the blind!" whenever the blind planter is to put a bird down.

When not actually planting a bird, he should sit quietly in his chair. If he makes any noise, or stands up and moves about, he might attract the attention of a working dog, which could cause the dog to fail the test. Frankly, in a test that has a large entry, blind planting is a boring but necessary job. The blind planter doesn't get to see any of the dog work, and he must remain unseen and unheard while each dog runs. If the entry is very large, most clubs rotate two or three persons in this job, so that no one has to do it too long. A blind planter may take something to read during his long periods of inactivity. However, he shouldn't take a radio or anything else that makes noise, for obvious reasons. If two blind planters share the same hiding place, they shouldn't talk while a dog is working, lest they attract the dog with their voices.

When the marshal says, "Plant the blind," the blind planter should select a bird from his container, hasten to the designated spot, plant the blind, and then hasten back to his hiding place. He should select a bird in good condition, not bedraggled, with feathers missing, skin torn, or intestines hanging out. He should set any such bad birds aside for the marshal to dispose of later. The blind planter shouldn't dawdle on the way to or from planting the blind. He's holding up the show, so he should get there and then get back as quickly as possible.

If, while he's hiding, a working dog approaches him, the blind planter should remain motionless and silent unless otherwise directed by the judges or marshal. Above all and at all times, he should keep his container of birds closed, so that no dog can get into it.

Go-fers and Runners

Throughout the hunt test, the marshal will need people to run various errands, like "re-birding" the gunner stations, carrying messages between testing levels, bringing lunches for the judges and for the various workers out in the field, finding handlers who aren't around when their dogs are soon to be called to the line, and on and on.

When re-birding the stations, the runner should hold the container of birds well above the cover in order to avoid laying a scent trail as he goes along. Ditto for the thrower or blind planter who comes to meet him halfway.

HOW YOU CAN HELP

It takes an army of helpers to put on a hunt test. For example, to run a triple mark with a flier and a double blind takes the following cast of characters: two blind planters, two poppers, two control bird throwers, one live thrower, two live guns, and a marshal (plus perhaps one or two go-fers and runners). That's ten or twelve people, not counting the two judges! Normally, while such a test goes on in level 3, a pair of single marks is usually being run in level 1. That takes two poppers, two control bird throwers, a marshal (plus perhaps a go-fer), for a total of five or six people. If one of the singles is a shot flier, one of the poppers will be replaced by two live guns, upping the total to seven or eight people. Therefore, at one time, the club may have as many as sixteen to twenty members working.

When your club puts on its annual or semi-annual hunt tests, you should volunteer to help in whatever capacity you feel competent. Anyone who can run his own dog in a test should be able to act as a go-fer, blind planter, or popper. Anyone with the normal amount of training-group experience should be able to throw either a control bird or a live bird. Anyone skilled (and sensible) with a shotgun should be able to shoot live. The remaining jobs, namely, captain of the guns, marshal, and hunt test committee member require more knowledge and experience, but if you have that, you should volunteer for those jobs.

One final thought: If you aspire to becoming a judge someday, the experience you gain in these various jobs will help you understand hunt test mechanics more completely. That will help you make optimal use of the facilities available in your judging assignments. It will also make you appreciate everything a club does to make your work as a judge go smoothly.

Chapter 11

So You Want to Be a Judge

The typical handler, at some point in his hunt test "career," gets an itch to become a judge. For many, it's an opportunity to contribute positively to the sport. Some would like to try a few new ideas that have stirred their imaginations, ideas they've never seen tried, ideas that would seem to have merit. Others want to right some wrong they feel they have suffered running under certain judges. For example, they may feel they've encountered too many trick tests and want to show the world how to set up straightforward but challenging tests. Or they may feel that certain judges have nitpicked their dogs into nonqualifying scores and want to show the world how to judge reasonably and fairly. Or perhaps they feel that many judges overdo the "just like hunting" theatricals and would like to show how to conduct solid hunting-type tests with far fewer dramatics. Or, on the other hand, they may feel that many judges slight the "just like hunting" props and procedures and would like to implement their own pet ideas for the betterment of the hunt test world. Or, or, or.

Others, frankly (and sadly), see judging as a gigantic ego trip. For them, judging would be a big "promotion," a giant step up the status ladder, one according them public recognition of their understanding of the sport.

For still others, the urge to judge is a form of me-too-ism. One or two people in their training group are judges, which makes them feel that, in order to become full and equal members of the group, they need to take up judging.

Thus, you shouldn't be surprised if, after earning a title or two, you begin to dream dreams about judging. Once you get that urge, you will almost certainly start moving in that direction, consciously or unconsciously, openly or subtly. My advice? As soon as you're properly qualified, go for it! Pursue that dream, but do it calmly and rationally. Hunt tests always need more good judges and, who knows, you may turn out to be one of the best in the game. You may be asked to judge all over the country in multiple formats.

But before you accept your first judging assignment, please ponder the following two sayings. They can help you become the first-rate judge that you dream of being. The first saying is for beginners in the sport. The second is for all judges, prospective and practicing.

FOR BEGINNERS

If you want to judge real bad, you'll almost certainly judge real bad.

Over the years, I've known a couple of rank beginners who had a far greater interest in judging than in learning how to train and handle their dogs in hunt tests. I met the first such guy at one of my retriever training seminars. He had never trained a dog in his life, nor had he ever handled any kind of dog in any kind of formal event. The dog he brought to the seminar was a middle-aged, totally untrained beast. I tried to help him with his training problems, but all he wanted to talk about was how he could become a hunt test judge. He seemed to want mostly the prestige of being recognized as a judge. (A few actual judging assignments would have lowered his estimate of said prestige significantly, believe me!) Fortunately, as far as I know, he dropped out of dogs altogether, so he never inflicted his ego on poor unsuspecting handlers by judging a hunting test.

The second guy was more persistent and far more clever. An incompetent trainer, he never successfully trained a retriever to even the lowest hunt test level. However, he politicked within retriever clubs in his area and eventually became president of one. In that position, he wheedled his way into judging assignments. His judging career didn't last long because too many handlers began refusing to run under him. No club can afford to lose money on event after event because of low entries. When he was no longer invited to judge, he departed the retriever world and went into obedience. There, too, he became a club officer without adequate dog training and handling experience. However, he never judged an obedience trial, because the rules there require extensive handling experience for a judge's license. He didn't stay long in that sport either. I have no idea what hobby interest he's now pursuing, but I'd bet he's president of some club somewhere and he's probably judging that activity, at least temporarily.

Both of those horrible examples occurred in the early days of hunt tests. Since then the sponsoring organizations (AKC, UKC/HRC, NAHRA, and CKC) have implemented their respective sets of minimum requirements for judges, which have eliminated most of the totally incompetent judges. However, even today an occasional misfit slips through, at least at level 1. Here I speak of someone who, after earning his first level 1 title, attends a judging seminar, and immediately seeks judging assignments in order to "make my dog's title more meaningful." How does he go about doing that? He sets up ridiculously difficult tests and then pencil-whips any dog that somehow survives through the last series. One hears about such judges now and then, and I once had one as a co-judge. That experience was a nightmare I'd gladly forget, if I only could.

Until a person has extensive experience as a handler, he shouldn't even consider accepting a judging assignment. He most certainly shouldn't try to politick his way into judging. If he does, he may achieve quick fame, at least locally, but his judging career will be short, and not fondly remembered, even by himself.

Years ago, long before we had hunt tests, many retriever clubs had an informal but excellent "school" for prospective field trial judges, in the form of frequent "fun trials," in which the more experienced members took turns judging. When a newer member began succeeding at a certain level, the club would give him a chance to judge in these fun trials. Most such novice judges made typical greenhorn mistakes, like setting up tricky tests to impress everyone with their cleverness, or nitpicking the dogs' performances to demonstrate their great knowledge of canine errors, or perhaps even putting on (sometimes humorous, sometimes infuriating) "airs" of self-importance. However, since these weren't licensed trials, where the threat of formal misconduct procedures control outraged handlers, these novice fun trial judges had to suffer the wrath of the handlers and club officers whenever they erred too flagrantly. A few such judging assignments either frightened the novice away from judging altogether or smoothed his rough edges and helped him become a competent judge.

Here's one mild example of this "educational process." Back then, a pair of newbie fun trial judges (not including me, honest!) set up a mark that fell on the crest of a hill in a way that allowed a dog that was well within the area of the fall to disappear from sight. There was a pond about fifty yards beyond the hill. Many handlers grumbled, but one young pro uttered a classic "stinger" to the judges as his dog disappeared over the hill. Turning to the judges, he said very dryly, "If you hear a splash, you'll know he's out of the area of the fall!" Ouch! With that comment, the pro pointed out very clearly and succinctly to the green judges that they had set up an un-judge-able test! If you can't see a dog when he's where he has every right to be, how can you judge him?

I started judging in our local club's monthly fun trials, and I made plenty of mistakes. Consequently, I got a well-deserved "earful" several times before I settled down and started judging dogs instead of trying to wow the world with my fantastically clever test designs.

On the other hand, during those early fun trials, experienced club members wouldn't allow anyone to bulldoze a green judge. Once, when judging a fun trial derby stake, I set up a straightforward and widespread water double in which each mark fell on the far shore of a pond about seventy-five yards from the line. One salty old pro began berating me for setting up a test too difficult for his string of derby dogs.

"Look!" he fairly growled, "I've entered several clients' dogs that are only seven or eight months old. They can't do a test like that!"

He continued in that vein a little too long for one experienced member, who finally interrupted him and said sarcastically, "The puppy stake was yesterday! This is the derby!"

The pro muttered, "Okay, I'll run your lousy test!" And off he went in a huff. He was right that several of his dogs couldn't do the test, but most of the dogs entered did at least okay.

Those fun trials were a school of hard knocks, but they did weed out those who were unwilling to learn from their own experiences. They also polished those truly interested in becoming competent judges. Very few clubs seem to have such programs anymore, which is most unfortunate. If your club doesn't have frequent "fun hunt tests," you might suggest initiating them. It not only will help educate judges, but also will furnish all members and their dogs with formal practice sessions in which they can prepare for licensed hunt tests.

Lacking such a club program, your training group can simulate this form of judicial education. During certain training sessions, you can let the inexperienced members take turns setting up tests. After a newbie sets up a test, but before the first dog runs it, the more experienced members should evaluate the test and explain any problems they see in it. Then the "apprentice judge" should adjust (or replace) his test before anyone runs a dog on it.

The organizations that sponsor hunt tests (AKC, UKC/HRC, NAHRA, and CKC) offer judging seminars that are most helpful for prospective judges. All four organizations also encourage "apprentice judge" assignments for prospective judges. In such assignment, the apprentice "judges" a licensed hunt test with two experienced judges, compares notes with them, and so forth. Of course, the apprentice's scores aren't used in the dogs' official score, but the experienced judges do look them over and evaluate the apprentice's judgment from them. This is an excellent way for a person to find out whether he's ready to judge or not.

FOR ALL JUDGES

There are two kinds of judges: Good judges and judges who want to be remembered.

Years ago, I heard this gem from Guy Fornuto, who said he had heard it from another judge years before that.

Anyone with a modicum of experience in retriever training can set up tests so difficult, so complex, and so tricky that most of the dogs entered will fail or at least do miserably. As mentioned above, many years ago, when I first started judging our local club's fun trials, I erred thusly, at least for a while. I found, to my great surprise, that I was wowing no one and aggravating almost everyone, sometimes even those whose dogs were successful. When the winners criticize your tests, they do get your attention. Fortunately, the club was patient with me, and I finally figured out that those fun trials were about the dogs, not about showing how clever I could be in setting up tests. Thus, in the years since then, when judging hunt tests, I've tried to set up straightforward, doable tests. However, since competition doesn't sort the dogs out in a hunt test, I've given qualifying scores only for solid dog work. This approach hasn't received universal approbation either, for some handlers think that just picking up all the meat should merit a qualifying score. However, I can shrug such complaints off with a clean conscience, because the disagreement is about the dog's work, not about the validity of test itself. (If there's any message in this, it's that judging is a thankless job, as I've pointed out often already.)

At a hunt test, the judge's role is similar to that of an official in an athletic event. No one buys a ticket to a football game, for example, to see how clever the officials are. As long as the players follow the rules, the less visible the officials are, the better for all concerned, including the coaches, the players, and the fans. An official who would showboat in order to "be remembered" will almost certainly be remembered by everyone there, but not in a kindly way. Fortunately, few such officials ever make it out of the peewee leagues or even last there very long.

Judges who want to be remembered invariably try to set up "impressive" tests. Some even like to hang their own name onto their pet test inventions. You'll hear such a judge say, "I invented this test last year for the such-and-such event, and it impressed everyone there so much that they started calling it by my name. This embarrassed me a little at first, of course, but the name stuck, so even I use it now." Yeah, sure.

Good judges set up straightforward, easy-to-understand tests that satisfy the rules and include enough meat to test the dogs. You'll probably never see a good judge set up a test totally unlike anything you've ever seen before. He may combine various tried-and-true test features in an endless variety of creative ways, but he's unlikely to show you an absolutely "original" test. To let the dogs show their wares, he doesn't have to. All the features needed to test the dogs appropriately have been around and well understood for about 100 years now.

Judges who want to be remembered often become theatrical performers at the line. They dramatize their explanations of the hunting scenario *ad nauseam*. I've seen such judges spend several minutes walking vigorously back and forth, waving their arms, and raising and lowering their voices emotionally while explaining each test. They continue performing for the handlers and gallery while the dogs are running. They might involve each handler in some sort of theatrical role-playing. For example, as each handler comes to the line for a cold blind, such a judge might say, "Hey, ol' buddy, you're late! I've already downed one drake mallard that fell way over there by that stump. Think your dog can get it for me?" And so on. Such a judge sometimes tries stand-up comedy, especially between dogs. Happily, I've never seen one resort to sarcasm.

Good judges explain their tests clearly and briefly, and then answer handlers' questions, also clearly and briefly. Thereafter, they seem to become invisible at the line, allowing everyone to watch the dogs work without a distracting judicial performance.

Judges who want to be remembered inflict their pet peeves on the handlers. For example, I once heard a judge in a level 1 hunt test tell the handlers that, as far as he was concerned, if the dog drops the bird into the handler's hand at the line, it fails to satisfy the requirement for delivery to hand. He expected each dog to sit at heel and hold the bird until the handler grasped it and commanded the dog to release it.

Good judges go by the rules and common sense, adding no little flares and flourishes of their own.

And so on. If you want to be a good judge, meditate frequently on the proper role of a judge. He's not the star that everyone came to see. The stars are the dogs. He's not even a supporting actor. The supporting actors are the handlers. He's more like the stage manager, who never appears on stage but makes sure that all hands (guns, gallery, handlers, and so forth) do what they should do when they should do it. He makes everything run smoothly, without making the audience aware of his presence.

What would be the highest compliment a handler could pay a judge at the end of the day? It would run something like this: The last dog has run the last series, the rosettes have been passed out, and everyone is relaxing at the hunt test barbeque, when a handler approaches one of his judges and, not realizing that he was a judge, asks him how his (the judge's) dog did and what he thought of the tests. That is the level of inconspicuousness for which every judge should strive. Of course, such a thing could never really happen, for the handlers necessarily know who judges their dogs. They see the judges before each series, during the judges' instructions, and then again every time they go to the line to run their dogs. Thus, the above scenario is purely hypothetical. However, try this little experiment: If that happened to you, how would you react? Would you feel complimented that you were so inconspicuous, or would you feel slighted that you weren't recognized as a judge? If the latter, you might have a tad too much of your ego tied up in your judging. Think about it.

Final thought: Since it's clearly impossible that, at the end of a hunt test, any handler would fail to recognize those who judged his dog, no judge needs to "perform" in any way in order to be remembered. In other words, every time you judge, you will be remembered, one way or the other. Whether you'll be remembered favorably or unfavorably is entirely up to you.

Appendix
Important Contacts

ALL-BREED REGISTRIES

American Kennel Club (AKC)
5580 Centerview Drive
Raleigh, NC 27606-3390
Website: www.akc.org

United Kennel Club (UKC)
100 East Kilgore Road
Kalamazoo, MI 49002-5584
Website: www.ukcdogs.com

Field Dog Stud Book (FDSB)
542 South Dearborn Street
Suite 1350
Chicago, IL 60605-1508
Website: www.americanfield.com

Canadian Kennel Club
89 Skyway Avenue
Suite 100
Etobicoke, ON M9W 6R4
Website: www.ckc.ca

RETRIEVER HUNT TEST SPONSORS

AKC Hunting Tests:
American Kennel Club (AKC)
5580 Centerview Drive
Raleigh, NC 27606-3390
Website: www.akc.org

Retriever Hunts and Upland Hunts:
Hunting Retriever Club (HRC)
(UKC Affiliate)
100 East Kilgore Road
Kalamazoo, MI 49002-5584
Website: www.ukcdogs.com

Retriever Field Tests (with Upland Hunting Tests):
North American Hunting Retriever Association (NAHRA)
P.O. Box 5159
Fredericksburg, VA 22403
Website: www.nahra.org

We hope you enjoyed this **Alpine** *title*

OTHER BOOKS BY
JAMES B. SPENCER

TRAINING RETRIEVER FOR MARSHES AND MEADOWS

Spencer's primary training book covers everything from puppy training and obedience through double marks and blinds.
ISBN 1-57779-007-3
$34.95

HUP! TRAINING FLUSHING SPANIELS THE AMERICAN WAY

Focusing on the characteristics of eight flushing spaniel breeds from a hunter's perspective, Spencer speaks to the prospective dog owner, the puppy trainer, and those doing advanced retriever training.
ISBN 1-57779-043-X $24.95

RETRIEVER TRAINING DRILLS FOR MARKING RETRIEVER TRAINING DRILLS FOR BLIND RETRIEVES

These books show handlers why and how to use traiing drills for perfecting the exercises.
$18.95 each or both for $32.00

POINT! TRAINING THE ALL-SEASONS BIRDDOG

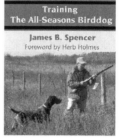

Clearly explained training methods will help you get your pointer out in the field as early as possible. Includes what to expect from various breeds, each training through training for competion, and how to teach those important birddog fundamentals.
ISBN 1-57779-059-6 $22.95

RETRIEVER TRAINING TESTS

The nuances of retriever training tests are explained, including handling techniques, how environmental factors influence the test, and 52 different test diagrams.

ISBN 0-931866-95-2
$18.95

1-800-777-7257
www.alpinepub.com